SWEETER VOICES STILL

An **LGBTQ** Anthology from Middle America

SWEETER VOICES STILL

An **LGBTQ** Anthology from Middle America

EDITED BY RYAN SCHUESSLER & KEVIN WHITENEIR, JR.

Belt Publishing

First Edition 2020
ISBN: 9781948742818

Belt Publishing
5322 Fleet Avenue, Cleveland, OH 44105
www.beltpublishing.com

Book design by Meredith Pangrace
Cover by David Wilson

CONTENTS

CONTENTS

CONTENTS

FOREWORD

Queer Heartlands

DOUG KIEL

The Midwest and Appalachia are both routinely identified as parts of the American heartland. What "heartland" means, however, is more than a little murky. Typically the phrase is used as a shorthand, quite often by politicians, to evoke images of small towns and white cisgender men and women laboring in factories and farms throughout the vast U.S. interior. In the popular imagination, the heartland is where "real" America can be found, where its traditional values and institutions are most cherished.

Garrison Keillor made a decades-long career out of satirizing, and often reinforcing, these one-dimensional perceptions in his writing and national-ly-syndicated radio program, *A Prairie Home Companion* (1974–2016). In each radio broadcast, Keillor described his fictional setting of Lake Wobe-gon, Minnesota, as a place "where all the women are strong, all the men are good-looking, and all the children are above average." Keillor's folksy caricature draws from a widely held notion that the heartland is defined by plain uniformity, the absence of difference. There are no LGBTQ people at Lake Wobegon.

It may seem a contradiction to be queer in a place that is so heavi-ly mythologized as the epitome of "normal"—and implicitly, straight and white—American life. *Sweeter Voices Still* reveals the heartlands as they tru-ly are: rich with queer human experience. They always have been, as Kai Minosh Pyle shows in their opening piece, "The Midwest is a Two-Spirit Place." From an Indigenous perspective, it is European ideas about gender and sexuality, steeped in Abrahamic religion, that are historically queer in the lands now known as the United States.

As many of the authors in this volume attest to, LGBTQ people in Middle America have often been made to feel out-of-place, like they don't belong in the region. "The prairie wasn't the place for boys who liked boys," writes Taylor Brorby in his piece, "Boys and Oil." Stacy Jane Grover's "Lan-caster is Burning" speaks to a similarly conflicted relationship to her home. After coming out as transgender, she notes, "I struggled, wishing to be a country woman, of the land" rather than being forced into exile. *Sweeter*

Voices Still is an act of queer worldmaking; it makes an important contribution to changing how the American heartlands are represented, signaling that it is possible for LGBTQ people to thrive in the "flyover states."

Throughout these pages, the authors bring the landscape to life, share memories of formative moments, and revisit the spaces that hold them. In stories and poems that span generations, readers are taken to piers in Michigan, a hunter's tree stand, fairgrounds on Independence Day, a dark stairwell where men cruise for sex, and bars that serve as an oasis of queer community, where the release of music and dancing can heal. Owen Keehnen writes of one such place, Irene's Cabaret along the Mississippi River in Quincy, Illinois, that for 36 years "was a melting pot of drag queens, leathermen, hustlers, lesbian farmers, bi-curious spouses, coeds, etc." *Sweeter Voices Still* highlights that not only do LGBTQ people belong in the heartland, but also they have long created safe spaces for each other, developing alternative forms of kinship.

The need for many LGBTQ people to seek out new, chosen families is underscored by testimonies in this anthology that detail struggles for acceptance in one's family of origin. Home can be haunting. Childhood memories about fathers and fragile masculinity loom large in this collection. As LGBTQ children begin to discover who they are and transcend social norms about dress and behavior, some fathers intervene to strictly reinforce binary gender roles, sometimes with violence and shame. Many, but certainly not all, of the mothers in these stories play a very different role as an important lifeline. In small but consequential moments that are captured in these pages, mothers are frequently a source of comfort, even a voice that gently hints it's OK if you have a secret. For some, particularly from earlier generations, open secrets about sexuality could go unacknowledged by families for an entire lifetime. In "A Tale of Three Seasons: Black Midwestern Lesbian Lineages," Jasmine Burnett writes about her great Aunt Betty, born in 1931. "My Aunt Betty never 'officially' came out," Burnett notes, "she simply lived and allowed you to arrive at your own decisions about how you thought she was living her life."

Throughout this book, the fear of judgement by God and family are among the most powerful forces keeping LGBTQ heartlanders silent and in the closet. This is particularly true for the most devout. Andriy Partykevich, for instance, writes in "Vichna Pamyat" about his journey into the priesthood of the Ukrainian Orthodox church, while also coming to understand his sexuality. "I knew I was gay, God knew I was gay, but the Church could not or must not," Partykevich writes. Similarly, in "Letter to the Prodigal Son," an anonymous author from Amish Country writes about admiring the courage of another gay man who left the community to live his truth. He eventually returned, however, and the anonymous author notes, "I brushed away tears, for I hoped you could make it out there." Partykevich held onto his own secret through more than 20 years of service to the church, but did ultimately leave the priesthood and married a man. Partykevich expresses deep regret, seeking forgiveness from his late father for having never come out while he was alive. Sometimes the struggle is to accept oneself; as the anonymous Amish author asserts so poignantly, "because our people won't forgive us, we must forgive ourselves."

The stories and poems that Ryan Schuessler and Kevin Whiteneir, Jr. have arranged here, with musical cadence, present the heartlands in a new light, moving far beyond one-dimensional stereotypes. *Sweeter Voices Still* is a remarkable achievement, providing a truly kaleidoscopic view of LGBTQ life in Middle America.

INTRODUCTION

RYAN SCHUESSLER AND KEVIN WHITENEIR, JR.

This book is about a place. A place home to innumerable stories. Some you know, recounted time and again around dinner tables and barstools, between raucous laughs and in hushed whispers. Others untold, or buried so deep they stir a familiar resonance you only recognize if you listen closely. Tales of family and friends; of love and hurt; of fear and joy in these places that we call home.

In recent years, much has been written about the Midwest and Appalachia. A lot of it was spent trying to map dark lines across the country's gray areas; a vain attempt to establish where, exactly, they were at all. Being queer often gets talked about in a similar way: only when someone hubristically tries to define it do we see how blurry its borders actually are. Both have long struggled to be understood, or at least respected; their narratives have often been created by someone else. The ways we fight for Midwestern, Appalachian, and queer representation are quite similar, yet, too often, mutually exclusive. But here we are—Midwestern and Appalachian queers—existing in the middle in more ways than one. Taking this moment to tell our own stories.

The stories in this book come from as far east as Buffalo and as far west as the Bakken; as far North as the Upper Peninsula and as far south as Oklahoma. These are the homelands of Indigenous nations, so numerous we cannot name them all here. They remind us not only that this land was stolen—a history too often taken for granted—but that their lives encompass so much more than trauma. They remind us that they are here, and that many of them are queer, too, in ways and words beyond the LGBTQ acronym. We implore you: as you celebrate your stories and ideas of these places, honor and turn your eyes to theirs.

Both of us are from this place. Ryan grew up in Missouri before moving to Chicago as an adult. Kevin was born and raised on Chicago's South Side before moving to very-rural Wisconsin for college. We come from very different communities—racially, economically, spiritually. But both of us identify somewhere within the expansive LGBTQ acronym and have never felt the need to leave this place because of that. On the contrary, it is why we envisioned this book.

The Midwest, Appalachia, Rust Belt, Great Plains, Upper South—Lower North?—whatever this place is called, is a queer place. It always has been. Its cities, farms, hamlets, reservations, suburbs, mountains, grasslands, forests, rivers, lakes, swamps, cul-du-sacs, dirt roads, and highways have birthed and shaped queer lives in all their beauty and mess. They are the backdrop to the existences we continue to fight for. Despite what American history might have you believe, this place is not a place from which queer people must always flee to find or save themselves. The queer people here do not exist only to serve as "blue dots" within "red states." For every story about the kid from Iowa who steps off the bus in Manhattan, ready to "finally" live, is a story about the kid who was already living in Iowa. This book is about that kid and has been written by people like them.

Within this book's pages you will find queer voices you might recognize: established and succesful writers and thinkers. You will also find voices you might not—people who don't think of themselves as writers at all. You will find Black voices, immigrant voices, undocumented voices. You'll find voices that have been scorned by a church, and voices from within a church; you'll find Hindu, Muslim, and Jewish voices. You'll find voices speaking in Spanish, Cherokee, Hmong, Somali, Ukrainian. You'll find an unsigned letter from Amish Country. You will find stories that spread a kind of contagious glee. You will find stories dripping with a familiar pain, and yet whose voices are sweeter still. Sweeter all the same. You'll find sex, love, and heartbreak and all the beings we meet along the way: trees, deer, cicadas, sturgeon.

You will find these truths within these pages: Transgender women and men are women and men, bisexual and aesexual people are real, "they" and "them" can be singular pronouns, Black lives matter, sex work is work, and you don't have to go to a gay bar to be gay—and it's okay if you do, too. In this book, we say "queer" a lot, but know that word means different things to different people and can be painful, especially for our elders. We see you, too.

Most importantly, though, we hope that people see themselves in this book's pages. Every queer person's life is punctuated by the moment when they first recognized someone like them in a movie, book, or TV show. For some, that has yet to even happen. Even if this book is not that moment, we hope it is in service to a future where that moment is so normal you don't have to hope it will happen at all.

This book is for the kids from Missouri, the South Side, Lac du Flambeau, Amish Country, the Allegheny range, downstate, the U.P., the Sandhills, and so many other flown-over places, so that they might have an easier road.

The Midwest is a Two-Spirit Place

KAI MINOSH PYLE

OZAAWINDIB | THE HEADWATERS
Lake Itasca, MN

Me, standing there. Sunlight hot on my shoulders, water running ice-cold on my toes. I'm reaching for the bottom of the stream—and it is a stream, right here, not yet a grown river—where the rocks are smoothed down from time. Not as much time as you would think, though. The hidden dam has only been here for a hundred years, built by the programs meant to boost the country out of the Great Depression in order to make the headwaters "beautiful." Something more momentous, something befitting the greatest of *American* rivers. Something that would draw in the tourists. They call it the Mississippi in English, but in the original languages of this place it never had only one name. Fiercely attendant to its twists and turns, the Dakota call it Ȟaȟáwakpa and Wakpá Tȟáŋka, the Anishinaabe call it Gichi-ziibi, Misi-ziibi, Wiinibiigoonzhish-ziibi, Bemijigamaag-ziibi, and finally at the point where it flows into the lake of deemed its origin, Omashkoozo-ziibi.

Two hundred years ago the woman named Ozaawindib would have known these names well enough to take those white men to the headwaters. In the journals that keep the accounts of the white men's guided tour, they call her a brave man. Brave she surely was, but she was no man. Even the would-be American lover who scorned her thirty years earlier wrote in his book that all the Indians called her woman, no matter what kind of body she had been born with.

Those Americans called that white man the discoverer of the headwaters. They celebrated it as a scientific achievement. Ozaawindib, she knew his real goal, Mr. United States Indian Agent. Coming to insert himself into contentious Anishinaabe/Dakota relations—it was better for the U.S. if the Indians didn't fight. Easier to make treaty, take their beautiful land.

Two hundred years later I am standing there, toes in the riverbed. A transgender Anishinaabe relative on stolen land. I am standing there and I am saying her name.

WAZOWSHUK | THE RESERVATION
Mayetta, KS

I found her in the pages of an old ethnography. Named three times over, I choose to remember her as Wazowshuk. That American name, the one they wrote in the census, is a deadname to me. To her wealthy employer's daughter she was Louise, a name given in jest but received with joy. Fifty years after her death that employer's daughter, a Potawatomi who married white, remembered her to an anthropologist, called her a queer fellow, gave her a girly nickname. A cute joke, but when the family came back from abroad she was wearing skirts. The grandmothers called her m'netokwe. Spirit woman. They still knew those old roles, those ceremonies for people like her. In 1970 anthropologists were still calling her berdache.

What I know is, "Louise liked *she*"—the closest thing I've ever seen to preferred pronouns recorded in the archive. I know she didn't like to wear beadwork. She liked her employer's daughter's hand-me-downs, white women's clothes, that stuff coming out in the Sears Catalogue. I know she like to ride sidesaddle in dresses through the Kansas fields. Even when those rich girls laughed.

Her father, born before the removal, wasn't raised on those plains. He walked the Trail of Death to Osawatomie and made a new life on the reservation. It was just open prairie grass then, the land giving their tribe its new name. The 1880s came around and both his children got allotments, Wazoshuk male in the eyes of the government, but it was only a matter of time before that land was taken too. Not even a death date in the records to mark her passing. Nothing but a memory written down in these dusty pages.

RALPH KERWINEO | THE CITY
Milwaukee, WI

It was a scandal at the turn of the century: a woman passing as a man. A Black Indian passing as white. A jilted ex-wife. Interracial bigamy. The story had all the fixings, but it's hard to find his voice recorded in newspapers that lied, put words in his mouth to suit their readers. Hard to even know to say *she* or *he* but I try anyway because s/he deserves better.

Cora was born in her ancestral homelands. Her mama had watched Potawatomi Territory become Indiana, married a Black man who'd come up from the south. It was safer with other brown folks, them and their in-laws the only dark faces for miles around. Cora got out of there as soon as possible: nursing school in Ohio, a job in Chicago, a new life in Milwaukee. It was a regular tour of the Midwest, those old Potawatomi lands. They looked different now though, all stone and smoke and street noises. Milwaukee was where he and his woman Mamie started calling him Ralph. Life's a tough business for a pair of brown girls, they said.

It worked just fine for a while—until he ditched Mamie for a white girl. Well, you can bet that she went straight to the police, ratted him out, and that was all the press needed. Newspapermen at the doors of his jail cell hounded him. There was a court case, tears and brash defenses, a recalcitrant repentance. When he got out he toured the freakshows for a while. Man-woman they called him.

It's hard to say what happened after that. A few years later they found him again in Menasha undressed in bed with a pretty girl, men's trousers rumpled on the floor. They charged him with vagrancy, too. What I want to know is this: how can you be a vagrant in your own homeland?

A Harvest

Pinckneyville, IL

EVAN WILLIAMS

I eat beef—only
if it's bourguignon—no
less than the best to snap me out of my neanderthal
veganism I'd settle for
some seitan screwball squirrel
atop chickpea children maybe
kidney shaped candies composed of ground up peach
fuzz or some tempeh
tiny Tim trophy sweetened with ten buck coconut-fur-

sugar I am a neon-bikini hunter up in the tree stand
admiring an ivory-hued tower through a scope
on a rifle made by Hasbro firing bullets made of balloons
current corpse count: zero and standing
still if I am merely to holler *bang*
might as well look to
kill a freaky-freekeh-fanatic-flamingo oh flesh farmer
brother where art thou skinny
jeans and sensible shoes
oh brother haven't you heard
camo is not yet back in vogue: here

is man as man was designed to be
the one who fears meat-eaters and meteor dust in his scars is
me the real backwoods biddy
singing some showtune ditty oh please
ain't I pretty like Snow White like Alice or her kitty or Gretel
who left home and grew past sibling sinew stew size

I sleep in sheets of leaves and live on
the nutrients of the soil's pity take root a petunia begonia
forget me not I have a rifle
made by Hasbro and bullets
made of balloons I am
bound to your cadaver city.

What Happens at the Woodward

Detroit, MI

AARON K. FOLEY

A former coworker of mine posted a photo of herself on Facebook with a bruised, swollen eye, and cuts on her face still fresh. Shortly after came another status saying she had been hit in the face with a bottle during a fight. And then after that, another status saying that it had happened at The Woodward and, according to her, the staff had not been helpful when she lodged a complaint.

How a cisgender, heterosexual woman got caught in a bar fight at a gay bar should be a mystery, but not in Detroit. She had posted that others had told her about The Woodward, and "that's what happens there." Those folks, unfortunately, are right. That is how it is at The Woodward Cocktail Bar, located at the intersection of Grand Boulevard—we call it "the boulevard"—and Woodward Avenue just a few miles north of now-bustling downtown Detroit.

As a black gay man, The Woodward, which largely caters to men (and once a week, women) like me, is supposed to be my scene. I've been gay-clubbing and bar-hopping in New York City, Chicago, San Francisco, even as far away as Milan and Melbourne, and there's no place quite like home. (Well, except maybe Atlanta.) I resist the word "urban" at all costs when it comes to describing anything black. It's what the bar is described as when compared to other gay bars in Metro Detroit that play top 40 music. The Woodward plays hip-hop and R&B, and not just the generics. It plays eastside Detroit hood shit, hustle—a very specific Detroit-style brand of line dancing, trap, jit, baby-making jams from ten years ago that still sizzle, and, on specific days, old school from way back in the day. There are no dance remixes of Adele. There are house remixes of Kelly Price.

It is the hub for Detroit's black gays, and perhaps the last time a white gay was there—except for the charming Russian behind the bar—was when, on a whim, I brought along the one I was dating at the time. (People stared at us crazy, by the way—My bad.) The drinks, despite being made with liquors found anywhere, are unusually strong, and have reached mythical status in their city—never more than two if you want to make it out alive. And speaking of the bar, it famously only takes cash, even in the age of Square and other such money-exchange methods. The younger gays are on the dance floor in one room, while the older gays are in the front room at the bar. All ages can be found smoking weed on the patio.

I've flirted here, and hooked up later, as a single man. One of my exes flirted here, and likely hooked up later now that I think about it, while we were together. I once ran into his cousin here coked out of his mind. I've ran into guys who, like me, were closeted in high school. I would see regulars here for years who'd turn up dead later, announced via Facebook. While working in the mayor's office of Detroit, I brought our very-recognizable-in-the-public-eye chief of staff here for the first time. Another co-worker I took for the first time learned the hard way about what happens after two drinks. Everyone's got a Woodward story about the good times. Everyone's also got a story about the time they had to evacuate the club because of a fight, got caught in the middle of a melee in progress or the stampede out, or, once in my case and more than once in many others', dodged bullets from gunfire outside.

We've got a culture of violence at The Woodward that everyone's quietly accepted since, well, as long as I can remember. It's not like it happens every single night. It doesn't. But there's always the risk of a fight breaking out on the dance floor—or in one of the parking lots—over some dumb shit. "He was looking at my man." "He stepped on my shoe." "He think he cute." "He owes me money." There's never a good reason. It's just how it is. It may be the strong-as-hell drinks. It may be because we're from Detroit, a city that for all its greatness, has been mired in violence for as long as anybody, young or old, at the club has been alive. It may be petty gay drama. But whether we accept it or not, our relationship with The Woodward is complicated.

I think about where The Woodward fits into Detroit's larger story a lot. As a majority black city where, for decades, a significant part of that population has lived in poverty, it can sometimes be survival of the fittest. You have no choice but to be forgiving of people who have always been disenfranchised and put into circumstances out of their control. If black Americans have always had the short end of the stick during our time in this country, many Detroiters have had nothing at all to grasp onto. So we fight, physically. We grow up knowing how to fight for our lives, and in the case of many gay men, perhaps knowing how to fight for that before having to defend yourself against someone calling you a fag. It's just the way it's been in Detroit, and that carries over to The Woodward.

I don't think, however, The Woodward has kept up with the change in LGBTQ culture around it. At a time when the community has moved more toward community in the face of adversity, even if that community is, frankly, still fractured along racial lines, it seems more and more that The Woodward prides itself on being reflective of Detroit and only Detroit—to a fault. So much of a fault that we just look away from the fights and come back the next weekend. Except now, Detroit feels like it's moving on, seeing a resurgence after years of decline. And there's a larger conversation about the changing demographics of the city that's happening alongside this renewal.

For all its faults, The Woodward is very much Old Detroit. People have never fought at the new gay bar downtown by the RenCen, the first new gay bar to open in the city—and actually last for more than a year—in more than a decade. But that bar is also very downtown, and often very white. There's something nostalgic about a bar that only takes cash when everywhere else is striving toward Apple Pay, but in a city where many people may not even have the means to open a bank account, it somehow feels accessible. Another gay male coworker of mine notes the history of the pre-fighting Woodward, about how back in the '80s and well into the '90s, it was a space where the kinds of house music that Madonna and other musicians would take mainstream first flourished, and how that history should be preserved in the face of gentrification, which may or may not be, depending on who you talk to, rapidly moving in The Woodward's direction.

The Woodward sits at the end of the QLine, a much-derided light rail that runs 3.3 miles in each direction from the center of downtown to the edge of New Center where the bar is. Despite many criticisms of the train itself—it's slow, it malfunctions, it's generally faster to take a bus, ride a scooter or even walk—the property values along the route have risen. More new housing and retail are being built along Woodward. The old coney island across the street, from where those bullets I once dodged flew out when a guy fired his gun at another guy and broke the plate glass window, has closed. There are more white people in New Center than I've ever seen in People still pack The Woodward night after night. But a common horror story in Detroit is longtime businesses shuttering or changing identity when a landlord buys out, or prices out, a tenant. I tried to contact the owner or a manager of The Woodward to find out where they stand, but getting a hold of that information is a challenge. Half the time someone might pick up the phone, half the time they'd say call back another time. But then, I think about the fights.

Sometimes people say to keep Detroit as Old Detroit is to keep as many elements of Old Detroit there as possible—including our violence.

I've joked on Twitter, the same way people told my old co-worker who got her eye busted open, that there's always a fight at The Woodward. Part of that is self-deprecation as a member of Detroit's turbulent black LGBTQ community. But another part of that is defense, in a weird way. What would Detroit be without The Woodward? Would this place become another stale top-40 gay bar that, like that infamous one in Chicago and probably everywhere else, explicitly bans hip-hop as a subtle way to keep the black people out? Would it even be a gay bar at all and just become another overpriced cocktail bar with drinks made with fresh herbs, Japanese whiskeys and revived spirits du jour? Do we, or I, worry too much about the fights because of what the white people might think? Like, "oh look at those thugs fighting again, that's so Detroit." Or should we keep The Woodward as is, fists and all, as defiance against the white gaze?

It's complicated, just like Detroit is complicated. So I guess this is what we'll have to do in the meantime, which is what I've always done. When you go, don't leave your mind vulnerable to bad decisions by drinking too much. Keep an eye for the exits, and know when to make an exit. Stay behind the brick wall that backs the old hardware store next door if you hear gunshots. But, I guess, always have fun. I never mean to put The Woodward down. I've had way more good times there than bad, and I'd wager we can all say the same. That's just what happens there.

To Love the Horseman of War

Cleveland, OH

DOMINICK DUDA

I was forged in the likeness of steel & violence,
a bona fide swordsman impaling the soft pink
of any man I could wrap my hands around.

No origin is bloodless, the body unfurling
from the epicenter of its own roar & want
in a stampede of wounds. I've swallowed whole cities,

pressed lip to skin & made scab, thrift store
thaumaturgy. Does that arouse you? I'm their babe,
their bitch, glitterbird uncaged. The sun sets

when I tell it to set. Sure, they always want romance,
eventually, but I can't tarry. The gunpowder's
all rubbed off & I'm too wet to spark. *Where's the towel?*

I've got to go. There's a thousand faces in this city,
there's two thousand eyes waiting to eat me alive.

crusty midwest demi femme, mapped

Mequon, WI and Chicago, IL

KEMI ALABI

my father's open palm, drum taut, all war song.

                                    crown of lye, barrette & braid.

two chords plucked out my mother's throat,
wrapped in foil, hurled off a lake bluff.

                                    sink full of the boys' dishes
                                    & my wet, shriveled hands.

            all this, sea:
                        bruise blue, ghost thick.

& there:
                                somewhere between chicago & home,
                        my third skin scorched onto a highway,

                pipe tucked in my boot,
gina's breath singed to my neck.

the sin of her,
                        my first good meal.

                        the entire tongue.
                                every finger & lash, sweet lightning.

            whole body, gospel.
        whole mouth,   cauldron.
            whole heart,   witch witch witch.

                                & there,

       land:
           a bed I built myself,
            fresh country.

& there,
     sky:

         endless choir
                of cocoa &

              rose &
                 my name.

Lancaster is Burning

Lancaster, OH

STACY JANE GROVER

I see a city marked by flame. On East Main Street, General Sherman's childhood home stands as a museum. Every day pick up trucks with confederate flags in the back windows blast by in mushroom clouds of diesel smoke. The city takes pride in being the birthplace of the man who cut across the South leaving only ashes in his wake. The story of the great field burner and the many legacies fire left on this city have been seared into us since childhood. Ebenezer Zane blazed a trail from Pennsylvania to Kentucky, founding the city. The first Anchor Hocking glass factory burned to the ground and resumed production only six months later, naming their most famous product line Fire King. The Fairfield County Fair—the longest continually running fair in Ohio—was famous for such events as "Racing by Gas Light" and the "Lake of Fire." I carry these histories with me as I wander through town. I see them everywhere.

Down the street, the Grandstand in the fairgrounds smolders. The grandstand, built in 1909 and featured in the finale of the 1947 film "Green Fields of Wyoming," was destroyed by arson in one night. As I stare at the rubble, I remember the words of George Ward Nichols, Sherman's aide de camps, as he saw Atlanta burning: "A grand and awful spectacle is presented to the beholder in this beautiful city, now in flames."

Across town, smoke looms large and black above Anchor Hocking's clamshell as the factory burns again. Firefighters on extended ladders pour water from hoses to quench the billowing flames. Seeing them, I am re-minded again of Sherman and his response to President Lincoln's call to send more troops to fight the confederacy; "Why, you might as well attempt to put out the flames of a burning house with a squirt-gun."

On King Street lay the remnants of a house exploded by a basement meth lab. The spires of brick towering over the blackened hills of rubble carry fragrant memory upward from the stones below.

On the occasion of this fortuitous homecoming, of seeing my birthplace in flames, I ponder the nature of self, of place. I haven't inhabited—

occupied, lived, been present or taken up space in—this town for years. And while the town never fled the corridors of my bodily memory, I fled it. The landscape of Fairfield County, Ohio sprouted the seeds of my imagination, helped them take root. I created my own worlds in which myriad lives were lived among the very real rich and varied Appalachian characters with whom I shared my life. My father levitated at church. My mother foresaw her grandmother's house burning down. My grandmother braved a barn fire to save a horse. The women of my family were sensitive, always seeming to know more than what was visible, impossibly wise to me as a young child. I dreamed of inheriting their strength and wisdom, and in many ways, I did. I wore and played how I chose, hidden by the trees and valleys that surrounded me, unencumbered by the terrible burden of gender. Without any references to compare myself to, without any knowledge of others who felt or thought like me, I assumed everyone did. I had the vague sense that my queerness was a mark, but it was mine and I wore it well. It took the shapes I formed it in, filling the empty spaces of fields, dancing in the shadows between forests, falling freely down rolling hills deep into the sandstone valleys below.

I was a shy girl whose mind was shaped by the geography as much as the geography was irreparably being shaped around me. As trees were removed for roads, fields for houses, barns for garages, so too was my own imagination replaced by an overgrowth of new information. I encountered stereotypes of the rural women I idolized that portrayed them reductively as strong, fierce preservers of rural culture, matriarchs with otherworldly attachments to the land, or as poor victims, battered, subservient wives struggling to raise children. The best of them were the beautiful but dumb, available girls with strong sexual appetites. I inherited a new way of seeing from these negative portrayals. I began seeing the women around me differently. I began seeing myself differently, too.

When I came out as transgender and searched for a community, I struggled, wishing to be a country woman, of the land, that place of undefined gender, to not leave the landscape behind for my new-found identity. But I did not want to be a victim, battered, subservient. I didn't want to endure more than I had endured. The small queer community I found told me I had to leave the suffocating myopia of the countryside to experience true freedom, and deaths of Brandon Teena and Matthew Shepard—the first and only visible manifestations of queerness I had encountered—only reinforced in my mind that the only good queer in the country was a dead one. Rural life and queer life were simply incompatible. With nothing to hold onto, no strength to reference, I gave up trying to affirm myself, burying my feelings in the soil deep beneath sedimentary layers of red clay and limestone. I felt trapped, as though the mountains were threatening to collapse and bury me beneath them. I had to get away, to put enough distance between me and this town, as if my problems were tied up in the landscape, the sacred forests of my memory, as if the geography that shaped me was suddenly my undoing.

I moved to the city where I found not the expected freedom but constraint; not the promised anonymity that would allow fluidity in my expressions, but constant surveillance. I inherited a new queerness, on that was now a mark I was told how to wear, shaping me into contours I didn't recognize. I was what was restraining my transformation, and in order to grow into the shared vision of metropolitanism that would lead to my salvation, I had rid myself of all that marked me a bumpkin. The knowledge of myself absent of a referent to reflect back all that I wasn't. That seeing stars was a part of being, that horizons were literal, that backwards was a direction that most often lead to family, that sunsets couldn't be blocked by anything but mountains and only if one decided not to climb them. These things I could not bring into the dusty confines of the city, the brick and wire and concrete hardened any permeable part of my mind, kept out the climate that shaped me, the person I had been amongst the fields and trees and valleys of my childhood.

Walking through this landscape now, my memory map morphs as landmarks I encounter remind me not of a place in stasis—mythically free or myopically restrictive—but of an ecosystem in constant flux.

In each ecosystem fire behaves differently, and organisms within them have to adapt accordingly. The characteristics of how fire interacts with a given ecosystem is called a fire regime. Fires burn at three levels: ground, surface, and crown. Ground fires burn through the soil that is rich in organic matter. Surface fires burn through dead plant material on the ground. Crown fires burn in the tops of the shrubs and trees. Organisms that live within these regimes are either resistant, tolerant, or intolerant to these types of fires. The places within an ecosystem ravaged by fire range from freshly burned spaces to those fire left untouched for years. Sites burned by fire progress through continuous and directional phases of colonization, which are characterized by the vegetation that arise. After a fire, the seeds already present in the soil, or seeds that can travel quickly to the soil will be the first to regrow in the burned space. Different species of plants are capable of exploiting different stages in the colonization process, creating in the landscape patches of multiple species. The unique makeup of these patches is determined by the characteristics— soil, climate, and topography— of a place, characteristics in constant flux

There are spaces in town where fire has burned enough for me to inhabit. The antique store, the catacomb of consumerism's past, where beauty and embarrassment fetch equally dubious prices atop their unflattering, dust-drenched, wood-paneled crypts. I fit in here, somewhere between the state spoon collections, the mid-century furniture, the mannequins who, like me, stand strangely over-dressed, catching double glances by passerby's knowing the proportions aren't quite right. I can hide here amongst these queer items queerly out of time.

The coffee shop in the old hardware store on Broad Street with the décor more out of place than me, demanding more attention than I can garner. Giant paintings of Santa Claus praying in sanctuaries hang from the exposed brick, distracting gazes away from the tables in the back corner where I sit with coffee reading, unnoticed for hours.

The alley behind the old record store where I first kissed the boy with the blondest hair wearing orange parachute pants and candy bracelets who waited for me holding sushi. Shaded for over a century, thick moss meets brick street where few cars pass, and few feet bother to tread the uneven facade. I sit alone daydreaming, unburdened from the necessity of constant attention to my surroundings.

There are spaces where the fire has barely touched, where I can inhabit only fleetingly. Fountain square at night, where I can sit at and look up at the clock tower through the tree branches. The silence expands the city to be able to include me. I can't stay long, for daytime brings families, children, businesspeople, relational categories of existence that, when present, erase my own. But for a while, the water is all mine; the cherub faces gaze only at me.

In Rising Park, the green surrounding Standing Stone, where nature offers refuge, but also a seclusion that allows for violence. I hide off the regular paths, my feet finding comfort in uncertain terrain. The view from the mountaintop shrinks the city so that I'm able to include it within me. I savor what I can before moving on, careful to notice those around me.

The west side by the factories, in the "neutral ground upon the outskirts of the town where was neither town nor country, and yet was either spoiled." The gaps in the railroad tracks and power lines, the holes in the fences, the cracks in crumbling foundation gives me room to breathe, to think, to create. The isolation leaves me unprotected. I keep moving, never stopping long enough to be seen.

There are spaces where the fire has not touched, where I find little or no space. The grocery store, under the unforgiving incandescence. I go at night and park close to avoid the jaundice light of the parking lot, the groups of men and their cars gathered at the edges, the aggressive machismo brewing trouble. I hit the needed aisles with precision, never strolling with Ginsburg or Whitman, feet always moving, head always down.

Independence Day at the fairgrounds where the throng of bodies moving in close quarters squeeze out that which doesn't fit the mold. The combination of feverish nationalism and alcohol becomes a potent mix that never fails to combust. I watch from afar, reminiscing a youth spent sprawled on quilts staring past the red-chipped barn roofs into a coarse July sky.

The mall, the microcosm of the consumerism's worst traits illuminated by piercing fluorescence and hard, unwelcoming floors. The building contains my body, hyper-visible, unable to escape the gazes of others or the memories amassed in a decade of working here. I won't risk going.

I circle back through town breathing in the smoke from so many fires. The smoke has seeped into my hair, my pores, the fabric of me. The thick scent conjures faded bodily memories, summons in me the realization that no matter how I've tried to erase the traces of this place, the Ohio country has stuck like pollen to every inch of me. No matter how I've changed or tried to wipe the dust of wheat and corn from my being, I can't. The mountains have opened my senses to a different way of knowing, of being so that no matter where I go or who I encounter, I weave them into the quilt of my past.

The city weaves into a patchwork before me, the fires burning holes that provide glimpses of pathways regrown and growing, membranes seeping and spilling, the ecosystem pulsating, glimpses of eternity. I know the story of this place is not a linear trajectory, not the narratives inherited from my ancestors, the writing of will onto landscape. The land is the land is the land, and while it has never been open, it has opened me.

In Rising Park, four hundred people spread out under trees and by the many ponds celebrating the county's first Pride parade and celebration.

The unusually cool Ohio June—free of rain and its usual high humidity—helps celebrants relax, let down guards so readily worn, guards that often keep them from participating in, let alone appreciating, the daily spaces they inhabit. When possible, relaxing in the summer often brings anxiety, fear, and violence to those unable to buttress themselves inside away from other bodies and the necessity of light dress. The day carries a peaceful density cuts through the usual tension. No protestors come to intimate; no preachers on bullhorns come to shame. For an afternoon, the tension rages on outside the confines of these bodies melded in hill, shade and tree. And in the center of the park by the largest pond, a new tree sprouts in the shade of old ones, finding room amongst all that is already present, the genesis of eons of soil, climate, and topography, the creation of the flux.

Cyprus Pride

Columbia, MO

JOANNA ELEFTHERIOU

When I was thirty-two and a graduate student in Missouri, a Greek Orthodox priest would tell me that being gay was not a sin, but more like being born deformed.

It doesn't damn you, he said. *It merely keeps you from some of the pleasures of being alive.*

I did not think, at that moment, seated on the cushioned pew of a Greek church in Missouri, how little sense the metaphor made. Just as people with deformed feet cannot run, the priest explained, so gay people cannot touch the person they desire. I did not, in that instant, recognize the fallacy of comparing physical and cultural laws. I only watched the emphatic pumping of his shoe, as he kicked it out from beneath his cassock each time he said *club foot.* I did not, in that instant, think about the mountain Taygetus, whence the Spartans flung children who were born deformed. From that mountain, every Greek school student learns, children whose bodies did not match the Spartans' ideals of strength and health were tossed. When I was young, we had driven together up the slopes of Mount Taygetus and stood on the spot where, I'd learned in school, the ancients had left their infants out to die if they were born sickly, or imperfectly formed. My maternal grandmother was Spartan. From that mountain I imagined that if I had been born two thousand years earlier and deformed, I would have been taken to the mountain by the parents that had given me life, and left on its glistening limestone for my flesh to become food for the jackals and the hovering birds of prey. Some accounts insist that in Sparta infants weren't merely left, but hurled from the cliff, a brutal sacrifice made for the sake of the Spartan nation— for the strength and purity of the tribe.

I would remember Taygetus later, in the empty hours of spring break. But as I left St. Luke's that day, thoughts scattered like birdshot, I wasn't thinking anything yet; I sensed nothing but a blinding sun, and the heat of the steering wheel that felt suddenly foreign, and difficult to hold.

Father Michael's message was not a new one. Since I'd first apprehended a whisper of the erotic pull, I had received notice of my self as unacceptable, impermissible—exactly what the church hymns and prayers referred to in phrases like *dark pleasures of the night, impulses of passion,* and *turbulence of our flesh.* I had felt the impact, and incurred imperceptible, persistent, devastating damage. What was new was that it was said out loud, directly to me. For years I had been told implicitly that my self, as it was constituted, was a problem, a perversion, and that my bodily integrity was at the mercy of a culture that required its members to conform.

It's been three years since that conversation with my priest. My island has been awake for hours by the time I, in my Midwestern subdivision, rise and hunch over a laptop screen to wait for news. It is May 31, 2014, and on the other side of the Atlantic Ocean, Cyprus is having its very first Gay Pride Parade. Victorian sodomy laws remained on the former British colony's books until, in *Modinos v. Cyprus,* the European Court of Human Rights ruled that Cyprus could no longer keep a law that made sodomy punishable by five years in prison. I was fourteen when the court ruled in favor of Modinos, but Cyprus resisted decriminalizing homosexuality until 1998, when I was already in college. This is the Cyprus in which I spent my adolescence and half my twenties. This is the island on which I tried not to believe that I, too, was gay.

Between Nicosia's long rows of towering palms, a sea of people moves, rainbows on their chests and on their backs, *love* in three languages: αγάπη, *love* and *aşk.* Limited as I am to what I can see on my laptop's screen, it is impossible to tell which of the people are the Greek Cypriots, which are the Turkish Cypriots, which are the gay and which are the thousands of straight allies who have driven from all over the island for this parade. The island has been partitioned for forty years, and presence of Turkish Cypriots on the "Greek" side is radical in itself.

My friend Erika has ridden a bus from our town of Limassol into the capital, and when she calls to tell me she's arrived, I thank her for marching for me.

"I'm not just here for you," she answers. "I'm here for everyone." She tells me she can't reach the parade's starting point yet because members of a group called the Pan-Cypriot Christian Movement (ΠΑΧΟΚ) are blocking access to the parade. The police have formed a line to keep the marchers safe. The "Movement" pays lip-service to the rights of all Cypriots "Greek-Cypriots and Turkish-Cypriots, Armenians, Maronites, Roman

Catholics," but in practice advocate only for right-wing Greek Orthodox Christians. Until I started reading on my own, I bought into the perspective of my conservative Greek school books, which presented Greek Cypriots as the only victims of intercommunal violence, and the only ones who needed their rights restored. From that conservative perspective, the Turkish-Cypriot minority had not been oppressed, and Gay Greeks weren't really Greeks. In anticipation of the 2014 Pride parade, the archbishop of Cyprus made an official statement that homosexuality is, and has always been, an imported, foreign disease.

Today, all this is different. Today, the rainbow flags make gay Cypriots real.

Suddenly, I exist.

Children are raised up on their parents' shoulders towards the sun at the same level as the flags and the signs: *same love—equal rights*. Above a first story of adult bodies, the bodies of children, the rainbow flags, and the signs form a second story of hope: *homophobia harms you and those around you*. Another says *Kuir Kıbrıs Derneği*, or *Queer Cyprus Association* in Turkish. Another sign says, in Greek, *FOR THOSE WHO CANNOT YET BE HERE*. I'm sure it does not only refer to people like me, who live far away, in places where it's easy to hide out, easy to wear T-shirts from gay events, and say that I'm gay, because no one will hurt me. Rather, the sign also refers to those who are living in Cyprus, but would risk being beaten or put out of their houses if they were seen at the Pride parade.

I never thought it would happen, not, at least, so soon, not before my hair turned white and my sadness grew so heavy I could not find a way back. During my eleven years on the island, I heard the word *gay* every day and always as a slur. Much later, when I moved to my progressive Missouri college town for graduate school, I began to talk about my love of women, and to refer to myself using words that I had learned as insults. In academic circles of twenty-first century America, I was called brave. It was sweet to earn praise for speaking so uncomplicated a truth. I felt, however, that if I'd had real courage, I would not have left Cyprus, where being gay was hard, and where pride parades were not safe.

The counter-protesters carry no guns, only banners with words. I spot the word for hell in Greek, κόλαση, and in English, *disaster*, along with quotes from American demagogues and from quacks: *cannot be strictly genetic*. Some men peer over the policemen, bouncing in place, yelling, "Hey! Are there gays back there? Eh? Are there gays?" They begin to shove the police, who are in their riot gear. They are hit by the men carrying banners of Bible verses, nationalist tropes about the blood of Cypriot martyrs, and translated propaganda from right-wing America.

The helmeted police officers lock their arms. Priests in their long black cassocks and their cylindrical priests' hats try to stop the men with banners from beating the police. These clerics must not have realized that when they recommended banners that condemned gay people weeks ago, they were arming their congregation not only with words, but with sticks.

When a television reporter stops a man from the counter-protest to ask why he is there, the interviewee seems puzzled by the question, as if the reporter had asked why he was defending the country against an invading army. He answers with a question. *What are they trying to do? Proclaim their... their... perversions?* He doesn't understand why they —we — aren't hiding.

The appearance of videos and online reports on my computer screen slows as the parade in Cyprus comes to an end. Night has fallen in Cyprus and no one has been hurt. It is still daytime in Columbia and I want to watch more videos of religious, banner-bearing men. I want to watch even though it hurts. I will later ask myself what drove this compulsion, and why watching felt good. I will realize that it feels good to have proof that the hatred I feared was real. That this is what they do. This is what they would have done if I had let them see who I am. If I had been there.

When there is nothing new to watch on my computer, I go for a run in the humid Missouri heat. I think of my friend, the poet Carolyn Forché, who insisted that one person, one person's art, can change the world. The year we met, I explained that I was trying to decide whether to give up my Orthodox faith or renounce my love of women and remain celibate because there aren't any people who are both Orthodox and gay.

"Then you'll have to be the first," she said. I told her about the priest in Missouri and she said I should find another.

I'm running now, thinking of a run years ago when a pop song on the Cypriot radio said, *why don't you believe that I love you? Why won't you come back ?* And I, a teenager, felt it was God, speaking through the pop song, because he had noticed a hesitation in my prayer after a year or more of passionate, ecstatic prayer. I apologized to the pop singer (or Christ), and said I would come back. I wasn't yet aware, then, of my homosexual desire, but I had been feeling the resentment the church's rejection of that desire had produced.

Twenty years later, running on a Missouri trail, a trail that goes all the way to Kansas, I feel it again, someone asking *why won't you come back?* I respond to God with a condition:

You'll have to take me as I am. The girl I used to be, the girl willing to pretend she doesn't fall in love with other girls, she's gone. This is who I have become: a woman who sees the beauty of women as the brightest of all beauties. I can't love a God who doesn't love me this way.

I head back to the house, feeling like maybe that conversation changed something. It's getting so dark I can hardly see but it is still hot, so hot I feel different in my body, different about my body. The endorphin-ecstasy that takes me over while I stretch brings with it a new way of seeing. I see that there isn't love without body, there isn't *person* without *body*, that this *soul* I used to associate with love isn't real without the reality of bodies, of desire. I wasn't just scared of being gay—I was scared of the body that responded to women's beauty in ways my mind could not control.

When my sweaty self turns on my computer, I find that Erika has posted an image of the demonstration to Facebook, writing *for Joanna Eleftheriou and all others who could not be here.* For a minute, two minutes, I want to take down my name. I imagine my Cypriot neighbors shouting that I, a shameful deviant perverted lesbian, don't deserve to be called Greek anymore—I have brought shame upon my parents, and must not be allowed into Cyprus, not even to visit my father's grave.

I leave my name up. I turn off the computer, and go to sleep, changed.

A version of "Cyprus Pride" was first published in *The Bellingham Review* in 2018.

Jell-O Salad

Howell, MI

GABRIELLE MONTESANTI

Ask anyone from Podunk, from Backwoods, from Flyover. Find one of us redneck, white trash, Honey Boo Boo bitches. Talk to somebody whose dad wore a jumpsuit—either at the shop or in the slammer—and make sure their mama couldn't help with homework past the fifth grade. Somebody who never had their own bedroom. Somebody who thought the county fair was vacation and Hamburger Helper was some real gourmet shit. What I'm saying is to ask the Lowdown, the Nobodies, the Hicks and the Hillbillies. Find one of us and ask. We'll tell you about Jell-O salad.

Mine was cherry. Served in the glass bowl where Goldie died. Blueberries frozen like hail over a rocky pretzel wasteland. Cool Whip or mayonnaise to taste. Each year at Christmas, there were no chairs at the table, just a bucket of chicken and Jell-O salad for dessert. Paper plates, plastic forks, Grandma's crucifix looking down on it all.

I've crawled through caves under Naples and dodged tourists in Times Square, but I've still never found a space tight as Grandma's house. Cousin Cal always tried claiming the couch's armrest; he'd perch there and squawk cuss words until somebody told him to get the fuck off before he breaks the damn couch. Aunt Susan camped out in the kitchen in case anybody needed a cup of well water tea or an off-brand Oreo. Aunt Donna sat on the floor in front of the La-Z-Boy to clip Grandpa LeRoy's toenails, which were yellow and thick as quarters.

All nineteen of us cousins ate our Jell-O salad in the hallway, the only place we weren't underfoot. We dug out the fruit with our fingernails just to chuck it down the laundry chute, threw around funny names for our future kids, like Ankle Biter and Butt-Licker. Most of us planned on staying in Nowheresville, or we just didn't know we had any other choice. Cousin Jessica was perfectly content staying put even though she got called Hoebag by all the boys and Floozy by the gray-haired neighborhood gossips. Cousin Tony liked that his teachers remembered having his daddy in class and knew him as the most charming mailman in town.

Some of us cousins were I've-Gotta-Get-Out-Of-Heres. Cousin JoJo talked about how she was gonna marry the first rich man she met, didn't even care if he was an Uglyface. Cousin Chris fooled himself into thinking he would play for Detroit, even though he couldn't catch a baseball if it smacked him between the eyes. Mom once found a drawing of skyscrapers in the margins of my journal and tossed it out into the rain.

Every summer, Mom and Grandma shaved the dog with the same sheers Grandpa LeRoy used to trim his beard. They'd hammer a stake into the soft ground between the old chicken coop and the moss-covered Virgin Mary and tie Lucy to it. Mom put her in a headlock while Grandma went to town. A dull hum. Lucy's ragged breath. Tumbleweeds of fur carried off by white-throated sparrows. Every now and again, Mom would loosen her grip and half-shaved Lucy would run as far as the leash allowed.

What I'm saying is, I know what it's like to be tethered to Bumfuck, running in circles like an animal. It doesn't matter how far away I move or what City Slicker skin I try on. Nobody cares that I use ten-dollar words like *juxtapose* or that I *juxtapose* everything I am now with all the places I've been. Doesn't matter that I cough up extra dough so I don't have to wipe my ass with that thin-as-a-Bible-page off-brand toilet paper. Doesn't matter that I learned in college that Mr. Right is a Miss and now we're planning a Gay Wedding in a Gay City five hundred miles from Grandma's house.

Here's what matters: I keep a box of cherry Jell-O in the pantry behind the red lentils and the flax seeds. On days when I'm feeling like some kind of Posh White Whole Foods Biddy, I think about whipping up some Jell-O salad, but something always stops me. Maybe I'm worried I can't make it like my people. Maybe I'm afraid I won't like the way it tastes.

Lezbens

Viroqua, WI

JENNIFER MORALES

It's so easy for writing to become revenge. I don't mean this that way. And I apologize in advance for depicting my nemesis in this story as a toothless hick. I really do.

Last Sunday, Keren and I attended a picnic put on by a church we are considering joining. The first time we visited the church, the minister was away at a conference but we were welcomed cheerfully and generously by the deacons and laypeople.

We've been back a few times to—I'll call it Downtown Church—since then. The picnic was maybe visit number four for us, so we're getting pretty serious about this one. We've consistently enjoyed the services, especially the casual and very human way the minister interacts with her congregation, and the friendly congregants themselves.

At the picnic, Keren and I introduced ourselves to a few people, but when it came time to settle in with our hamburgers and salads, we sat with a husband and wife we had met on our initial visit. It was clear on our first meeting that they are both introverts, like us, so we thought we'd be safe from the exhausting work of small talk. Plus, I had noticed this couple had, like us, brought their own utensils from home so as not to use the plasticware on offer in the picnic shelter. Shy, environmentalist dorks, unite!

A fifth person was at the table and I sat next to her. She is a somewhat disheveled woman I had seen around town. Covered in rashes, awkward of gait, and thin of hair, she seemed like she was struggling with a lot of health issues. When I would see her, outside the library or walking down Main Street, I would always try to say hello, but clearly here at the picnic table she didn't recall my face.

Keren and I talked with the couple about our recent move to the area, our jobs, their family, their jobs, etc. Occasionally, I would talk with the woman on my right—I'll call her Bee—and she would tell me about her health troubles, her diabetic ulcers, the draining of the pus in her legs by incompetent nurses, all good lunchtime chitchat.

At one point, taking one of many sharp turns of conversation, she asked, "Have you been to that store downtown, Tulips?"

"Yes," I said. "We went in there a few weeks ago and looked around."

The store bills itself as a general store, with a little cafe, and some food, soaps, herbs, housewares, clothing, and gifts for sale. It was funny that Bee should bring Tulips up. Almost every local we have met has assumed we know the owners, the other obvious lesbian couple in town, but we don't.

Bee dropped her voice. "You know what they are, don't you?"

Uh oh. I knew where this was going, but I wasn't going to buy a ticket. "No. What?" I asked.

Bee looked me right in the eyes. (I'm going to mention here that she clenched her seemingly toothless mouth shut, because toothlessness adds to the ability to lock a mouth down especially tight, not because I want you to think any less of Bee for lacking teeth.)

"Lezbens," she said. (I'm going to spell it the way she said it. For accuracy. Not because I want you to think any less of Bee for mispronouncing words.)

I tried humor. "No!" I said, in mock surprise. Bee missed all the mock, but rode to town on the surprise.

"Oh, yeah," she said, nodding enthusiastically. She then told of some community function recently where she was offered a chair next to "one of them" and she refused it. "I'm glad I didn't have to sit down anywhere near 'em," she said. (I'll record that as "'em" because, well.)

The irony of her sitting next to me on the picnic bench sent a shiver of suppressed laughter through the rest of us at the table.

Bee went on a ways about the appropriate treatment of lezbens if you see them in the community. The couple tried, with somewhat heroic perseverance, to turn the conversation. The moment passed.

I looked at Bee. I sat with Bee. I listened to more pus stories. Then one about getting a prime seat at a music festival. Then one about an argument she had with her neighbor, leading to the neighbor calling the cops on her. Then one about the doctor saying her leg might have to be amputated.

I don't know if Jesus would have bothered to bring his own utensils to the potluck. But I'm pretty sure he would have sat with Bee and listened to her stories, even after she talked a bunch of trash about Galileans. He also wouldn't have mentioned the teeth.

The Bridge

St. Louis, MO

MARY MAXFIELD

The fourth fell on a Wednesday. "Ladies" night at the local gay bar. My wife, Melissa, and I had spent the day in her hometown, Belleville, helping her parents and avoiding "happy Independence Day" well-wishes. We were itching from new mosquito bites. We were itching in other ways, too, hungry for something more *us* than strip malls in oversized parking lots, chain stores decked in red, white, and blue.

We'd each grown up in southern Illinois, forty minutes from the other. I loved that we were from the same place, loved the magic of having met a girl in Virginia who'd grown up on the same strange diet of Jell-O salads, green bean casserole, and Ski. I loved it more because—like me—she'd found her way somewhere else and had no intention of a permanent return. When we did move back to the Midwest, her students teased her. "I said I'd never move back to Belleville, and I didn't," she told them. "We live in U City."

In other words, we lived across the river.

Growing up where we did, the river felt like a mystical barrier. Most people I knew would drive hours across Illinois but balk at spending forty minutes crossing the bridge into St. Louis. Later, I'd recognize the ridiculousness—and the racism—inherent in this attitude, but at the time, it simply transformed the city into a strange and fascinating mystery. On occasion, my uncle—who looked like a hippie Albus Dumbledore, from his long gray beard and ponytail to his bolo tie and Birkenstocks—would take us to the Loop, a strip of shops and galleries, punctuated by drum circles and street musicians. I'd stare, awe-struck, at humans bright with dyed hair and tattoos, remembering a girl who scandalized my grade school by dying her brown hair red.

Now, we lived a mile from that same strip. I had my own tattoo from the local shop. On weekends, Melissa and I biked Forest Park, the nearby mass of lawns and algae-covered lakes. Its landscapes immediately recalled those of my childhood: prairies lit with moths, still waters bubbling with unseen life. On the south end, the highway broke the illusion of countryside. Across the river, I was somewhere else.

That Fourth of July, Melissa drove us to the Grove, a stretch of Manchester that functioned as the current gayborhood. It wasn't a gayborhood as I imagined one: bears and butches walking their dogs, coffee shops soundtracked by spoken word. It was, instead, a series of gay and gay-friendly bars that generally awoke after my bedtime. Still, the rainbow and trans flags lining the streets relaxed my shoulders. The "Black Lives Matter" signs in the windows pushed me further into relief. Here, Melissa and I could hold hands across the table, dance, pretend freedom felt everyday. No small thing, anywhere.

That night, though, we were feeling bitter. We'd spent two years trying to find community—volunteering at the local LGBTQ community center, weeding the Trans Memorial Garden—only to introduce ourselves, once more, to the same impenetrable clique of queers we'd already met five times. We'd set up a meetup group for other local queer folks wishing to make friends. The Facebook page had taken off, but each offline invitation crashed and burned. We'd extended another invitation tonight and could already see the tumbleweeds taking shape. Instead, I sat alone at a high table. Melissa ordered drinks. Nearby, kg lang—the women's folk rock tribute band we'd come to hear—set up on a makeshift stage. They'd moved inside, away from the screeching cicadas, in anticipation of a storm. I sat sweating inside the screened-in porch, waiting for my gin, and staring at the Table.

The Table was impossible to ignore. It stood feet away, on the other side of the screen, near the outdoor bar. The Table was actually a collection of tables, haphazardly arranged into one organism. Around it, an improbable number of lesbians perched on stools or leaned on those who did. The night had barely started, and I sat alone, watching another lesbian, another lesbian, and yet another lesbian join this nearby group. Each one caused the assembled crowd to cheer, erupt from their seats and share a hug. I opened and closed apps on my phone, grateful when Melissa returned with my drink. Grateful for someone to know, and something to hold.

"How do we get *that?*" I asked, nodding my head toward the crew of butches, femmes, and queers behind us.

"We don't," she said. "They're full."

Around us, the music started. My gin and tonic tasted strong. I moved my straw in circles, trying to stir the bitterness smooth.

Then the music started, and my foot tapped, in spite of me.

Last Call at Irene's Cabaret

Quincy, IL

OWEN KEEHNEN

My heart broke a little when I read the news that Irene's Cabaret had closed in late 2016 after 36 years in business. I was a regular there, ass planted on a bar stool until closing, probably a few nights a week for a couple years.

I remember the nightly last call for alcohol: "Ladies, fix your make-up."

The first time I walked to the address at 124 5th Street, I discovered a boarded storefront painted black with a small sign affixed to the wood: *Enter in Rear.* The same phrase was printed on the bar's matchbooks—twice. The second time I went to Irene's, the bartender (everyone called him Whoretta) explained the joke to me. "See here, it says Enter in Rear, like in the butt." Whoretta and the bar owner, his "uncle" Irene, were always on the prowl.

Back in 1980, I was a young gay thing, fairly naïve, and living in Quincy along the Mississippi. I desperately needed a place like Irene's Cabaret.

Reading about the bar's closing, I was surprised that Irene's had opened in 1980. I had been going there almost from the start, but even then the place looked as though it had been around for decades. The decor had a lived-in look. Irene had brought some French provincial furniture from home and created a little seating area in the game room complete with a gilded mirror. I remember the etched tin ceiling, the worn purple carpet, the dim red lighting, and the red-flocked wallpaper. There was a David statue adorned with a boa, a disco ball, plastic ferns, and mirrors along one wall. There were baskets of salty popcorn and a pickle jar. Overall, Irene's had a sort of riverboat brothel vibe.

Restaurant surplus tables and chairs surrounded the dance floor and to one side, a glowing diva-heavy jukebox—Della Reese, Dottie West, Streisand, Cher, Eydie Gorme, Miss Ross, Blondie, Patsy Cline, even Pia Zadora. On quiet nights at the bar Willie (aka Irene) would often hand me a few quarters, "Hon, go play something on that thing to make me smile."

That summer I also discovered that Irene and Whoretta lived in a bungalow behind the music store where I had an apartment on the top floor. My bedroom overlooked their backyard. I used to watch them, lying out in the blistering sun in their speedos slathered in a mix of iodine and baby oil—sipping cocktails, chain-smoking Salems, and talking nonstop while flipping through magazines. Some days they used foil covered double albums to get deeper coloring on their faces. Whoretta told me when folks saw her coming she didn't want them to see anything but teeth and the whites of his eyes.

Irene said the whites of Whoretta's eyes hadn't been visible for years.

"Whatever you say, you old hooker."

They were a family.

The article on the bar's closing mentioned that Willie/Irene had died in 2015. There was no mention of a nephew or Whoretta.

Irene and Whoretta weren't the first gay people I met in Quincy. I'd met several others, but most of those men were discreet "gin and Judy" bachelors who congregated regularly for cocktails and conversation in one another's homes. They were an odd blend of lechery and prudishness. Their words dripped with innuendo and, being young and cute, I was the focus of much of that attention. The "gin and Judys" embraced discretion, though everyone in town knew about them. They followed the unspoken rules of being gay in a smallish town.

Irene and Whoretta did not follow those rules. They embraced neither discretion nor tradition. Having a good time was their master plan. Willie told me that having a good time was why he opened the bar in the first place, "We all need a place to go for some laughs, some romance, and a little fun."

Irene's was where I decided to become a writer and where I honed the drinking skills that seemed a prerequisite for that occupation.

At the bar I fell in love with Kevin, my first "real" boyfriend. Kevin and I spent countless nights there playing pinball and pool, drinking, arguing art (ugh), and falling in love. We considered ourselves bohemians. We were going to join a commune someday. We were going to do so many things someday. Kevin is dead now, too.

Irene's was the focal point for queer activity in the tri-state area. People would drive there from Keokuk or Springfield or Palmyra on the weekends to party. It was a melting pot of drag queens, leathermen, hustlers, lesbian farmers, bi-curious spouses, coeds, etc. Every combination of LGBT was represented at Irene's most nights of the week. In the bar's crimson light we became comrades and friends, and had a lot of laughs.

I realized I was gay years before moving to that lazy river town. However, at Irene's I discovered that being gay could be about more than having gay sex. Irene's was where I realized that being gay could also mean being part of a community. After feeling like an outcast for years, I had no idea that being open and still having a sense of belonging was a possibility for me. The realization changed, and possibly even saved my life.

So many memories resurface at the thought of Irene's Cabaret. On more than one occasion, Kevin and I had wondered what any of us in the tri-state area would do without the place. News of the bar's closing made me consider the question again. I didn't have an answer.

A version of "Last Call at Irene's Cabaret" was first published in the *Windy City Times*.

diaspora

Chicago, IL

RIVER IAN KERSTETTER

at the pow wow, we _____
at the gay bar, we _____

I'm trying to say,
we carry the dancing
with us.

I'm trying to say,
there is color
and laughter inside.

families used to living miles
apart
suddenly in one room
touching.

Nature Poem

The Appalachian Trail

SARAH SALA

In 1988 Claudia Brenner and her girlfriend, Rebecca Wight, planned to hike a section of the remote Appalachian Trail in Pennsylvania. They encountered a stranger who shot both of them, killing Rebecca.

. . . .

For a little while, there was a black butterfly with us.

. . . .

X later claimed ~~he thought~~ he was deadening
~~what was~~ deer

. . . .

A universe ~~bullet wound creates a cavity that~~ expands and ~~then~~ collapses in the spli

atom it takes a summer's day bullet to blink

. . . .

X wept in his cell to learn a lesbian had survived ~~his horrific attack.~~
See you later, he called at the campground.

. . . .

Rebecca, that May afternoon, we ~~wept~~ reclaimed our bodies in the secluded thicket

when you drove your ~~galaxy~~ pelvis across mine

The same look you flashed the day we met

I felt a lifetime drain from Pennsylvania ~~the sphere~~

in seconds

. . . .

What was it made X think since he never found

love

~~he should X-out someone else's?~~

· · · · · · · ·

My dear, Rebecca: you bled out in a forest along with ~~me~~

our futures

I bound your words up in my chest ~~to a songbird~~
Get behind the tree. Your direction life-giving.

After ~~the massacre~~, I covered you in the blue sleeping bag

I ~~never~~ wanted you to feel ~~cold~~.

every drop

of my ~~damned devotion~~

hesitation

To leave you there, living.

· · · · · · · ·

Four blazing miles I retraced our trail like a love letter to the highway
scraped over fallen logs warding off the night

my skull smoke escaping the shooter's lips
a beehive of shock
an engine of surveillance

a white towel plugging my exit wounds

. . . .

X's reckless ammunition designed using calculations and data gathered
from previous testing
perfect for small game .22 barrel action rifle

. . . .

ER doctors

        threw me up against the ~~periodic table of elements~~

           odds

Rebecca, your parents cremated your remains

            before I ~~could touch your hair~~ left inten-
sive care.

After the murder,

        the third disappearing act.

"Nature Poem" was first published in *Women's Studies Quarterly* (WSQ)

On Our Nightly Walk, She Takes My Hand

Asheville, NC

JESSICA JACOBS

Across the dark street, the dance studio
is a brilliant lamp, a Cornell box

set to music and motion: girls hold each other
in swaying *pas de deux*, a phrase

first translated for me as *piece of God*.
That's wrong, of course,

but not entirely. For what is it to move in time
with another, to acknowledge and learn

a body beside your own—the dancing apart
and the final coming back

together—what is this if not
some kind of grace,

some human-sized serving of God?

Boys and Oil

Western North Dakota

TAYLOR BRORBY

1.

We play army at Tyler's birthday party. Cream the Carrier, Smear the Queer, King of the Hill—games boys on the prairie play to the swoosh of grass in afternoon heat. Something in the land pulls us towards violence. We tackle our friends, drive our hollow boned bodies into the hard dirt. One team holds fort atop the butte, the other down in the coulee. No mercy, no grace, forget what we learned in Sunday School. The trees echo with screams, cries that ripple across the prairie.

2.

They lived together in a tawny house on the south end of town, across from the Corner Stop. Ms. Voss and Ms. Leingang, the English teacher and the History teacher, volleyball coaches too—they shared a house together. One had curly hair the color of sand, the other straight black hair, typically tied in a bun. We lived two blocks from them before we moved, and my sister had them both in the classroom and on the volleyball court. Later, when I got older, I heard rumors about how they liked to linger in the locker room after games, talked with the players who stripped and got in the shower, washed the sweat and salt from their game-tired bodies. I only knew Ms. Voss and Ms. Leingang in passing—on my way to the library in first grade, marching in alphabetical order for Mrs. Sherwin. We scurried as the bell rang and high schoolers flooded the hallway. I remember that their smiles looked the same—gaps between their front teeth; big, warm grins, mild bemusement behind their spectacles. Later, Ms. Voss and Ms. Leingang moved, together, to a larger town.

3.

We'd peel around the pothole-riddled road, the Corner Stop the finish line—no stop lights or signs to get in the way. Like rockets launching into the sky, we slammed our legs down and up and thought we were headed for the moon. Waxy leaves twitched in the breeze as sweat slid down our faces. We blinked faster to keep it out. Tick tick tick snapped the playing cards in our tires. Jeans, stained with grass, wet and heavy from sloshing in the creek.

We ripped around the corner, the boys and me, heading home from base-ball, but stopping first for candy, except—wham—Cale went over the handlebars, knocked out his front two teeth. Like Chiclets stained red, they shined in the slant, mid-morning light. Stay there! we hollered as we peddled on, not knowing what Cale's parents would say, his sobs echoed off the tall cottonwood trees. That's what happened, the way it was, in our little town—each boy bound to the other, ready to sever the cord when things got tight.

4.

I'm sitting at Grandma's vanity in Aunt Shelia's old room, while Grandma, fiddling with her pearls, says, *Would you like to have some fun, honey?* I nev-er say no to Grandma, the woman who peels my apples, cuts my bologna sandwiches into triangles without the crust—she knows I don't like crust. Grandma lifts me up and plops me on her lap. She unscrews the lid of a small vial, her acrylic nails click against plastic. *Do you like how my nails look, Taylor? Oh, yes,* I tell her. *I like them a lot. Would you like your nails to look like mine?* I close my eyes to think about it (we like to keep each other in suspense). I open my eyes and look into the bright light of the vanity. Grandma rests her chin on my small shoulder. *Yes,* I say. Grandma's white teeth glisten behind me. We sit and she hums as, stroke by stroke, my nails turn crimson—one, two, three, until all ten shine like bright little apples. And then Grandma holds my fingers, one at a time, and blows.

When Dad comes to pick me up, I bound up the green-carpet stairs like Daisy, my Grandma's black dachshund. Dad sees me, and I stop. I know that look. His eyes flash to Grandma. *Go back downstairs,* and I slide on my butt, bounce harder and harder on each step because I know I've done something wrong. I go sit in front of the vanity and stare into the mir-ror. *Mom, I have one son and one daughter, not two daughters.* Each word a jolt as I sit in my small chair, holding my cheeks with my fingers, as I begin to peel the paint from my nails.

5.

Tex ambles down Oliver Prairie Avenue, shaded by elms. He holds a paper bag in his sun-tanned hands. Cody and I are practicing t-ball, my Louisville Slugger over our right shoulders. We try to wind it in a circle like Kirby Puckett, before unleashing hellfire against that little ball on a stick. Usually, we miss, then look back to make sure the other isn't laughing, and try again. Today, Cody cracks it, a line drive right at Tex, who catches it. Does he giggle or cackle? We pull our caps close to our eyes and kick at the grass. Tex saunters toward us. *You have to get it from him. You hit it.* I push Cody towards Tex, who looks as big as a barn. *Sorry, Tex,* Cody says, and Tex stretches out his arm, pockmarked from cigarettes. He lets the men down at the Western Saloon put out their smokes on his scaled skin, one butt for each snifter of bourbon. Tex nods, grunts something into the air, and moseys along, step by step, and we turn to practice once more, to dream of the Major League, of getting far away from here.

6.

A sunny day in June. Baking day. Grandma wants my help. I climb the stool, roll up my sleeves, and place my hands on the cool counter, faded flaxen from years of rolling and flouring, whipping and baking. I push my chef's hat back to keep it out of my eyes. Grandma stands behind me, her liver-spotted hands hold mine, roll the pin back and forth, back and forth, spreading the dough like a rising lake. Her voice crackles in my ear, *A waltz, Taylor, it's a waltz when you bake.*

We're making sugar kuchen, Grandma and me, while her chokecherry tree shimmers in the afternoon sun. Everything dances at Grandma and Grandpa's—the house of polka, the home of hugs and laughter. Grandma, a small woman, her shoulders heavy from years of hard work—farming and children and cooking and butchering. The loss of her third child, a boy, Keith at three months. I never hear her say his name.

But, still, we dance. Mr. Welk and his *wunnerful wunnerful wunnerful* in the background. Grandma hands me sugar cookies to smash, the crumbled crown atop our thin dough, the sweetness in the sugar kuchen. And Grandpa comes through the garage door as I hop down for a hug. He smells like fish as he kisses Grandma.

I climb back on top of the stool and begin to whack and smack cookies, breaking bits like porcelain teacups. *Here are our little Champagne Ladies to dance a polka with us.* And they're off, Grandma and Grandpa. They spin in circles, whirl before me, Clarinet Polka in the background. A half-century of marriage twirls in front of me, and it seems that the world changes as an accordion plays in the background, a little sugar in the air, some sweetness in the room.

7.

Mom drops me off at the Civic Center for art class. Me, eight post-menopausal women, and Vern, our art teacher. Elfish, wire-browed, Vern, at sixty, is my height in junior high. Easels dot the cold, white room, and the radiators begin to rumble as we rub our hands. The women are ecstatic a boy is taking art lessons.

Vern and I go into a storage room, filled with faux wooden tables and gray metal chairs—somehow, it feels like a butchering room. Vern flicks on the projector where we place the picture of a brown trout I want to sketch. Vern turns the dial. In and out of focus goes the trout, a blonde creel next to its plump body. Vern looks as if he's about to tell ghost stories when out comes his pencil—a slash here, a mark there. Streaking across the bumpy paper, Vern's eyes narrow. I watch his hands, colored with pastel; his gaze never leaves the image. He steps back, holds the pencil near his mouth as his other hand, free, goes limp at his side. And I wonder if he knows, wonder if he can tell. A boy and a man, making art in a dim-lit room on the prairie, silence between them, and the door—

8.

We grapple, Cale and me, wrap thin arms around each other's heads. Wrestling, it's what boys do, and we sway back and forth like bluestem in the breeze, try to throw the other down, try to wrap our feet and pull the other forward, make him fall onto the hard brown carpet. That's what we want, to be on top, to hold each other in place, to do a Full Nelson, or a Chicken Wing, or get on the backside, wrap legs around stomach and pull—we want breathing to be hard, to whisper, *Hurts, doesn't it?* We don't do Stone Cold Stunners, but we'll body slam each other on the couch. We don't do

Rock Bottoms, but we'll do a Sleeper Hold. It's our way to show we're men, to show that, if we want to, we could hurt each other.

In second grade Cale and I played ball-tag, just the two of us. I kept getting the ball, hurled it like a stone at him, kept yelling, *Tag, you're it!* and then ran and got the ball again. Over and over, tag, tag, tag, tag. And finally, Cale, the larger, slower friend, picked up my baseball bat, whipped it like a tomahawk. When it knocked me back into the cold grass, I yelled, *Jesus Fucking Christ!* for the first time.

But now, in eighth grade, our bodies have changed. Stronger, lower voiced, we push harder, sweat more, our faces crimson. Cale plays ball, runs track. I do speech and practice saxophone. But today we toss and tumble, and when I pin Cale we both see it, can't unsee it—that our bodies have changed, and mine has betrayed me.

9.

In eighth grade Corey Hintz grew baseballs in his arms. In swimming class I had to turn away, had to keep from fading into a daydream—how he'd wrestle cattle into the cold mud, hold them down, arms locked around their head, hot iron pressed into their velvet coat, branding them for life. A small coal in my gut told me to look away, told me that the prairie wasn't the place for boys who liked boys—that's what we teach rural children. To be true, move away; find a home elsewhere; move along like a turtle slowly scraping away soil to reach the river, where you belong—someplace, not here. In eighth grade the boys lifted weights, and I changed quickly in the locker room, kept my head down as they snapped towels at testicles, cackled with delight. I kept swallowing the coal even though it hurt, hoping, one day, I'd find it turned into a diamond.

10.

My bright blue socks a dead giveaway. I stop at Liquid Assets for a drink, just a drink, I tell myself. It's a quiet night, soccer on one screen, the Twins on the other, couples whisper quietly in corners. I pull myself to the bar, and the bartender, a young woman, college-age, wearing a low-cut tank, says, *Sugar, what are you drinking?* I look at what's on tap and order a beer. I break my rule, going out drinking at night, alone.

It's maddening—surrounded by flares, metal testicles swing from hitches, t-shirts captioned Goin' deep and pumpin' hard or Frack that hole. My left hand quivers, I bring my beer to my mouth. Cool relief, cold safety. Something to ease the sad story of this place, Dickinson, North Dakota, the latest Boomtown USA. What the heck, I order another as my feet swing under my stool, bright blue breaks the drab décor of this room. Two men in cutoffs play billiards, remind me of The 19 in Minneapolis, though this is no bar to pick up men, no place of refuge in the storm of boys and oil and money and sex. I ask the bartender where the beer is from, *Beaver Creek Brewery in Wibaux, sweetie*. She likes calling me sweetie. Wibaux, Montana, a skip over the border, a place—Grandpa told me in childhood—where you could get married at sixteen. *What's the beer called?* She looks up from washing glasses and I notice her eye is purple-yellow, Redheaded IPA. *A redhead for a redhead*, I say, and take another swig.

Two's enough and I push back my stool, pay my tab, thank the waitress. I push open the door and a sting of diesel hits my nose. I look up at the inky blackness above and wonder about the inky blackness deep below. Where is my home going, this land on fire—and I'm off the ground, flying, just like I always wanted to do when watching Mary Poppins. I hit the stone wall, hard, take a kneecap to the brow, hear a low fag ring in my ear. I reach for my glasses, not broken, somehow, and hear the roar of an engine, the smell of burnt rubber. It's a white pickup, that's all I know. A white pickup on an ocean of black oil.

Boys and Oil first appeared in *High Desert Journal*.

A Seed

Pinckneyville, IL

EVAN WILLIAMS

They are boys and camo-clad and male which is to say they are
Carrying rifles that our uncles would call sticks and firing bark
Bullets into the sky aiming for birds hoping their target wings might
Fold into their forms and land crystallized on the ground

a trophy. We are the first bodies over the bird
Praying it back to life, wondering how it was felled
By imaginary projectiles. We are threatened, told to go
Home; here is a place full of dark magic and lethal secrets given to Sunday-

Loyal lads, libidoed torpedoes, fervent future flesh farmers in a forest that
is pretend labyrinth
Blazing trails from Bible-belt-fastened back door to Beatitude ecstasy.
They are escaped Hansels who told us Gretels to stay home, out on a mission for the witch's head,
Marking the path back with screwball squirrel hearts and roger rabbit kidneys.

They are polka-dot and coconut-fur-faced hoping to grow away
From peach fuzzy. They now stalk somnambulant, carry rifles made of rifles
and imagine
Firing bullets made of bullets to pierce the pastor-professed-inanimate bark
brain of a bark beast.
What is the mark of man if not drawn in dominion?

We are sober, still blasphemous to sacred slaughter, tykes sitting in carpeted
rooms with clean clothes:
The little boys who grow up to be littler boys than before, a special breed
Who bemoans bee death in the face of a sting, who becomes man only by
chance.
When we shave for the first time our not yet coconut-furry faces, we shake.
Then,

They become men or execution exhibitionists directed to divine manhood
from brutality—
We all learned that the earth is a Golden Corral buffet and *every moving
thing that is alive shall be food*
For us—it was all created, all given to the hankerings of hunt-hungry hands
lustful for legacy,
They grabbed plates first, christened the feast, stored all excess in their newly beard-born bodies.

Now we are *starving,* lesser men for having shaven, *naked, hysterically* mole-
faced, we go hungry to
Our rooms, whose walls are all flowers grown in soil fertilized by bloodlust.
It's us, the petunias, begonias, daisies, and forget-me-nots who are
Seeds knowingly planted and tended to gently by the brutishly soft hands
of bear

Skin covered brutes with patience who forget not a thing, who are friends
with the witch and her head,
Who know her tricks, who did track their way back to her lair less for murder than for lessons.
The Gretels are at home, they said, *show us how to grow sustenance of sinew
from sweet siblings,*
Thus became they carnivorous cultivators of cowardly crop, culling those
who caress crying creatures,

Growing them to end in a golden crisp. All the way back to home, they did
Snack on screwball squirrel Hearts and roger rabbit kidneys, then took us
from our flower room and said
Be fruitful and increase in number; fill the earth. And the earth having been
filled
They subdued it.

Wonder Boys

St. Louis, MO

SAMUEL AUTMAN

Saturday mornings in 1977 in our North St. Louis household meant wiping crust from my eyes, climbing down the bunk bed, and rustling Chung, my sister, from her sleep in the bottom bunk. We knew Mama had placed either Corn Flakes, Cheerios, or Lucky Charms in plastic bowls the night before. Chung and I would immediately grab them and turn on the TV to watch ABC's *Super Friends*. I liked the cartoon because Wonder Woman, Superman, Batman, Robin and Aquaman formed a superhero alliance. Chung preferred *Scooby-Doo, Where Are You!* and *The Bugs Bunny Show*. Once the cartoons went off at about noon, the neighborhood kids divided up by gender, and hit the streets.

I played Nerf football in the street with the boys, our strategies and rhythms interrupted every few minutes by the hum of passing cars. We would stop, disperse onto either side of the street, then quickly re-gather on the black tar to pick up the game. Meanwhile, the girls played Double-Dutch jump rope, their orange and red Jelly sandals bouncing rhythmically on the sidewalk. Sometimes they play acted as a cheerleading squad, patting their hands and stamping their feet in unison while making cheers that sounded like rappers. "My name is Chung! Yeah. I am a Virgo! Yeah. I am super bad! With power! All here! Let's cheer!" In those days, the streets felt safe. We heard about burglaries or houses catching on fire, but youth and naivete insulated us from what was on the horizon for our neighborhood and generation.

One time I was outside riding bikes with neighborhood kids Mikey, June bug, and Tony when we saw Steve, a kid who lived across the alley, resisting as his father, Mr. Johnson, pulled him out of their red brick house, down the stairs, and onto the sidewalk.

"So, you want to be a fucking girl? I'll make you a fucking girl," Big Steve thundered, with a belt dangling from his fist.

"No, Daddy. I'm sorry! Please don't make me do this," he pleaded.

Steve was about nine years old, effeminate, and petite. He had wide cheeks and always seemed more concerned about his face and clothes than playing on the streets with us. His father, who had to have been in his early thirties, was the ideal goateed muscular man who sat around sucking down

Budweiser beer out of the can and watching the St. Louis Cardinals play on TV. During a break one time, he opened the bathroom door to find Steve, his only son, putting on lipstick. Big Steve exploded, making his namesake put on a yellow turban, white high-heeled women's shoes, and a red dress. He then smeared makeup and lipstick onto his son's face in an exaggerated way, making him look more like a clown than a girl. Hoping to drive this tendency out of Steve, he forced him to walk around one big St. Louis block for everyone outside to see him. So, Steve began walking around the eighth-of-a-mile trek.

"I'll make you a fucking girl!" Mr. Johnson repeated, becoming louder as they went

"But Daddy, I was just playing around," Steve said, tears, makeup, and lipstick commingling.

"Well, guess what? I ain't raising no goddamned sissies, so just shut up an' walk."

As boys who were nine, ten, and eleven years old, we all thought this was the funniest thing we had seen. We clapped our hands and howled with laughter. Tears of humiliation streamed down Steve's face. We kept jeering, but I was horrified at what I saw Steve's father doing to him. It made me wonder if this was the kind of treatment I would have had coming if my parents had stayed married.

Steve and I were friends when the other boys weren't around. We bonded around the central female protagonists who populated our TV screens, really cheesy ones like *The Bionic Woman, The Secrets of Isis, Electra Woman and Dyna Girl* and the short lived *Get Christie Love,* a black undercover detective. The one we loved the most was Lynda Carter's *Wonder Woman.,* The way audiences could see her clothing disappear as she twirled around as Diana Prince to become Wonder Woman. We loved everything. Her golden lasso that forced people to tell the truth. And her bracelets that made bullets ricochet. Wonder Woman reflected something neither of us had a vocabulary for. Steve was far more creative and fun than the other boys. I knew if the other boys saw me playing too much with Steve I could be pegged as a sissy. By then I had an inkling that Steve and I were alike but I didn't want to be associated with him too much because the boys in the Penrose neighborhood called him names behind his back.

"I always thought he was a punk," June bug groused.

"Yeah, I knew he was a sissy. Look at him," Tony said.

Steve walked from his house, westward on Anderson, south on Marcus, east on Bessie, my street, and north back onto Cintra. Like a swarm following the summer ice cream truck, a cluster of kids began to follow Steve on that blistering summer day. The walk should've taken less than seven minutes, but with this growing caravan of boys on bikes and skateboards, it was taking longer.

Cars slowed to a near halt, looking at the commotion surrounding Steve. Some honked in mockery. Just as he was about to walk the final leg back onto his street, a silver Fiat belonging to Steve's mother pulled up. She jumped out of the car, slamming the door shut.

"Steve, boy is that you?" she asked, frowning. "What are you doing out here like this?"

"Daddy made me do it."

A tall feminine woman with shoulder-length hair, Sandra shook her head and scowled at her husband.

"What do you have to say for your motherfuckin' self?"

Big Steve looked dumbfounded as he tried to explain that he had caught Steve putting on lipstick, but his hysterical wife interrupted.

"Well, do you want to tell me what the fuck goes on in this goddamned house while I am gone? What have you done to my baby?"

A few of the neighbors gathered on their porches. Word had spread through the neighborhood. She pulled Steve by the arm, quickly getting him onto their porch. She opened the door and dragged her son in behind.

They all disappeared into the house.

"Wonder Boys" was previously published in 2014 as "A Walk Through the Neighborhood" in *Black Gay Genius: Answering Joseph Beam's Call* by Vintage Entity Press.

First Kiss

Ludington, MI and Peoria, IL

CARMEN SMITH

My mind is stuck on Michigan piers.
Something so docile in the way the waves
slap in my memory. It is a breakwater,
with a lighthouse at the end. Sometimes

something so docile in the way the waves
break is the farthest thing from the truth.
With a lighthouse at the end, sometimes
the memory makes me cry again,

break. Is the farthest thing from the truth
the guilt? Stunned, I slipped into the bathroom.
The memory makes me cry again.
She held me in the bathroom and I sobbed.

The guilt stunned. I slipped into the bathroom
and heaved. I remember every single moment
she held me in the bathroom. And I sobbed
like heaven had cast us out. I was sure of it

and heaved. I remember every single moment
our lips lingered, wanting to speak warmth
like heaven had. Cast us out, I was sure of it—
my whole body felt wrecked on some shoreline.

Our lips lingered, wanting to speak warmth.
We imagined God, lapping as if after a storm.
My whole body felt wrecked on some shoreline.
The calm of autumn is repetition, wind heaving.

We imagined God, lapping as if after a storm.
Slap in my memory. It is a breakwater.
The calm of autumn is repetition, wind heaving.
My mind is stuck on Michigan piers.

On A Bridge

Joplin, MO

STEFFAN TRIPLETT

Here was a church I had gone to. Another there. And yet another there again. Pointing them out to Marc was an easy way to fill the silences. Each time we passed one that I knew, I kept one hand on the steering wheel, excitedly pointing my index finger through the glass. I struggled to find enough interesting things to do to fill an afternoon in my hometown: Scrabble, Starbucks, a tour of the mall, the little art museum. And now, the churches. That seemed to cover everything the town had to offer. I had planned the park as our last destination.

The two of us followed the sidewalk that weaved around the playground, like the one I bloodied in the fourth grade. Young and clumsy, I had tripped and slammed my face into a plastic hexagonal roost. I bit deep into my lip, teeth breaking and busting out. I was silent at first, then felt a stinging, saw the blood, and began to wail. *Is he gonna die from this?* a classmate asked my teacher. I told Marc this story, praying he wouldn't find me boring. I told him stories of all the times I'd been here before. How my grandmother used to babysit and take me and my cousins here—my *white* cousins. How friends and I still came here at night during the summer, swinging back and forth until we needed to make curfew. And about the time a nearby resident called the cops on me, suspicious of the young man in the car.

An invisible rope pulled my stomach toward him, though I made sure not to stand too close. I was seventeen and I remember thinking this is what a real crush feels like. I kept my hands in my black zip-up. In the nighttime, the light from the street lamps didn't reach this far. We followed the path to one of the only areas that was lit: the little bridge near the gazebo. He stopped in the middle of it, leaning against one side of the bridge. I mirrored his actions, leaning on the side opposite from him, unsure of what to do next. Waiting, I noticed the grass was still alive and green in December.

Then Marc stood up from the wooden rail. He was directly across from me, beginning to close the gap between us. Someone from the neighboring houses across the street could see us if they looked hard enough. Two hours earlier, Marc told me he couldn't live in a town so small, so conservative. You have to come to Kansas City, he said.

His hair was black and swirly, and hung out from under his beanie. The dark waves rolled around his forehead as he moved. This is where his heritage showed the most—the hair of his Mexican father. His skin was pale this time of year, lighter than mine, which had faded as well in these months without much sun. The trickle of the small, man-made stream looped in the background as the early Winter chill surrounded us. He inched closer as I stood frozen, watching him read my face. I could feel it coming—a moment played out in movies by pairs that didn't look like us. His eyes were looking right at me. Could he sense my hesitation? Was he scared like me?

I held his glance, then looked away, not knowing what to say. I kept my hands in the pockets of my hoodie and shifted against the rail. He kept smiling and I tried to see anything but lips. His jeans were dark and skinny, the same pair he wore when we met at that college visit a few months back. His figure was petite and I saw its edges defined in the layers that hung on his torso.

"I want to kiss you," he said.

My stomach squeezed into itself. I stood up straight and inched off of the rail. I thought about what to say, but no words came out. It wasn't a question. It required no answer. The space between us tightened as he moved closer. All feeling went to my temples and I watched the place where his words left pulling in like a magnet towards me. His smell surrounded me and I felt breath and body heat.

I felt a boy's lips on mine for the first time.

For a moment, I didn't move. I took in the shock and the feeling of this pink warmth. I tried to match the movements of his mouth. My teeth knocked his. I laughed for a moment then pulled away. He laughed too, then saw I was no longer smiling. "What's wrong?"

Looking down, I shoved my hands in my pocket, and headed back to my car in silence. He followed. I fumbled the keys and got in the driver's side. Marc got into the car and shut the door. He probed, asking what was the matter.

"I don't want to be doing anything that's *wrong*."

His mind worked for a response. Despite my hesitations, his presence made my heart flitter. "This isn't a sin," he pleaded, breath floating between us.

Wanting to believe him, I asked again about his youth minister, the one he said knew Marc was attracted to men, and said that *God wouldn't care*. He had told me this over instant messenger, but I needed this kind of affirmation now, and in-person—I needed to know that someone "connected to God" thought my feelings weren't wrong. But how could Marc know who to trust? Marc assured me that she did exist, that she indeed had said those things, that she was real.

He started kissing me again. Enclosed in the car I could smell his cologne. A little like vanilla, and a lot like the woods. He smelled like comfort and warmth. Smiling, his eyes were closed. I closed my eyes hoping to feel the same. How was Marc so comfortable being physical with someone else? Another boy? None of this felt real. I tried to let my thoughts drain as I focused on the feeling. But I was worried about the police and the park's curfew. I told him about the time the cops came, again. Urged him to come back to my house.

"It's your car," he said playfully, gently.

Heat filtered through the air vents as I started the car. We left the cold at the park, toasting up. While we drove back to my house, he reached for my hand across the center console. I turned up the CD I burned the night before, trying to impress him.

> *"I want to know your plans*
> *and how involved in them I am.*
> *When I go to sleep for good,*
> *will I be forgiven?"*

He told me I was cute when I smiled. I tried my best to remember the moment.

Back home my parents were already asleep. Marc was spending the night and driving back home early the next morning. We decided that we would watch a movie downstairs in the living room. He wanted me to choose. I fingered through my dad's collection in the laundry room cabinets. I chose *I, Robot*. Feeling a need to explain my choice, I told Marc how my dad and I were really into Sci-fi.

"I'm really into Will Smith," he responded. We laughed.

Where would I sit on the couch? He was sitting on one end while I put in the DVD. I thought about what I watched friends do with their significant others over the years. *Should I just copy what they would do?* I sat down in the middle. I wrung my hands in my lap and he, sensing my inhibition, immediately put his legs across mine. He was making it easy for me. I was thankful for this kind of kindness. I put my hands on his shins. We sat like that for nearly an hour while we watched.

"Are we actually going to watch it all?" Marc asked. He took my shrug as an invitation and moved his head towards mine. I looked away from the translucent robot on the screen and leaned in to kiss him back. I felt a little better. I ran my hands through his hair. It felt like cold silk. Almost like mine did when I was just out of the shower, but just a little smoother.

"Your Chapstick tastes good," he said. I figured he was trying to help me relax.

"I'm afraid my parents will hear," I told him.

He kept kissing me, and I tried to ignore thoughts of what my parents would think. He lifted his shirt over his head and put my hands on his chest. *God, I just want to enjoy this.* I let myself touch the hairs sprinkled across his chest. He assured me that it would be fine, we'd hear them if they were coming down. This would stay my secret. Here he was, a real boy in front of me. A real boy who thought I was cute and wanted to talk of an "us" and the things we'd do. The credits started to roll.

"Are you ready to go to bed?" I asked.

The TV silenced the room when I clicked it off, and we quietly walked upstairs. We brushed our teeth and I liked the image of the two of us together in the mirror. I peeked through the crack in the door to make sure my parents were still asleep.

In my room, I made a pallet on the floor and gave Marc the bed. I moved the Scrabble box left out from before dinner and pinned the score sheet to my bulletin board. As he watched he said he had a good time, that he was glad he came.

"Me too," I said. It finally felt true. I was really gay now. It wasn't like before. I wondered when we would be boyfriends. Maybe we'd pick the same school. Our parents could get along—we both had white moms. We both went to church. We could come out together. We wouldn't have to travel far for holidays. It made sense. I was seventeen. We talked about the stars on the ceiling that still glowed dimly. My room was small, something he noticed when he arrived. I thought about the sailboat comforter on my bed, a captain's bed, to save room. The shelves were lined with books from my childhood, board games and plush animals stuffed underneath.

"Are you really gonna go to sleep?"

The emotions of the day had exhausted me. I couldn't muster a response.

"Well I'll just come down there," he said, laughing.

Used to his pace now, this time there was no rattle of teeth. I felt his weight on top of me. I reached up and turned the lock, just in case. Between breaths I took in his smell of chlorine, still there from his weeks of swim practice. I held the back of his head, gripping his hair and skull. This finally felt *good*. It finally felt *right*. He moved his hands lower and I moved them back up. He asked if I was nervous to "do stuff" with a guy for the first time. I couldn't tell him the truth.

"I just don't want to do any of that tonight," I told him. I had prepared my response to this question in advance. I wasn't ready for sex, and I didn't want to let someone else take that from me.

We returned to kissing. "Well, it doesn't *feel* that way," he sang gently. He respected my boundaries. He wouldn't try again.

For years I had been ashamed of my body's response. I thought about Sunday school. A teacher telling us about his cousin who was HIV positive and how *God gave it to him, how he deserved it*. About the signs those men held that said God hated men like me. It was hard not to believe it when that's what almost everyone was telling me.

Am I gonna die from this?

Marc kissed me again before he moved back up to the bed. I stayed on the floor. After a while, I reached back up and unlocked the door.

A previous version of "On A Bridge" was published in *Kweli Journal*.

It's a Theme

Chicago, IL

JESSIE KEARY

I am fostering elaborate fantasies about a person I have spoken to exactly three times. Good for commutes on public transit and the minutes leading up to an herbal-supplement sleep. The fantasies bleed into dreams—a reality of sorts—and I wake up feeling pervy because I just want to know this person. Actually. I think. Instead—looping scenarios, cute ideas. Everything goes well. A hiccup is still sweet.

It's the same feeling I get re-watching the same show or playing the same song over and over and. Cozy. Doc says I need to pay attention. There's a crossover—the search for emotional validation gives way to emotional indulgence. Some shirk from certain feelings while I bask. Want to lie at the bottom of the bathtub and. Doc called me porous. Like a sponge, she said. You absorb everyone's feelings on top of your own. I know, I said.

If Plates Are Shirts
Are Milk Jars

Nashville, IL

EVAN WILLIAMS

then it's dawn or dusk or
some other time of dark
and you can hear him on the stairs
in the hallway in the kitchen—
hear him moving plates around
fixing something bitter
to your taste buds like coffee

without sugar and you're tired
under the fleece of morning or earlier
or whatever time of dark this is
when he steps out the screen door
grabbing the grass with his boots
taking hold of the hinges hugging it shut

quietly. You hear him beneath your window
walking away and you pray on your knees
in the dark of this time that
he's coming back. Or you pray

on your elbows that he's leaving
but you can't tell at this time of dark
when he walks through the gravel driveway
toward the cows or the road
for a split-second you hear him
choose the road;
you never heard him pack a bag in the kitchen
unless plates are shirts maybe
he did and dark sounds fooled
half-awake brains into smelling bacon as bitter—
sweet? Maybe

plates that are shirts are milk jars. Maybe
they're neither and really are just plates. Maybe
it's just impossible to tell at this time of dark.

If Plates Are Shirts Are Milk Jars originally appeared in the *Rockvale Review*

How to Operate a Hide-a-Bed

Chicago, IL

ROBERT L. PATRICK

Things happen for a reason. If you're at all like me, you would have just completed an eye roll. Things happen in threes. Another canard. Third time's the charm. That's the clincher, isn't it? Trying so hard to make sense of the randomness of life, we often cite these platitudes (you know you do, even as you kick yourself for saying/thinking any of them), but they do, momentarily take the sting out what may have happened even if it was the fourth or tenth time. Life is a series of often unrelated events through which we move. Here's one of mine.

Prologue

My first steps into the world of gay life were hardly tentative and yet now, when I consider the facts (as I remember them), it must have been like a drowning man to whom multiple life-savers had been thrown, but which he cannot reach—lots of flailing around. It wasn't as if there were a guide-book (which it seems to me that there still is not one, more's the pity, but who would write it?) I can see how, if I had been a different person, in different circumstances, how difficult it might have been to emerge from this time unscathed. At least my battle scars are well won in a 'you should see the other guy' kind-of-way. What I thought it was about was wrong, but there was no one to tell me what it should have been.

There were so many opportunities to be outed. The year before, with Claire and Kyle in my dorm room sitting dangerously close to where I had my stash of photos of hard cocks (just cock, no body, no head, no man to go with them; where had I found those in the cold frozen tundra of northern Minnesota I cannot remember, but nonetheless I made a collage of them and used it as a springboard for, when I was alone, masturbatory fantasies); the knowing look from Kip one day as we sat in a circle of friends smoking a joint. It was 'the look', the one that says, "I know who you are, you can't fool me; god, am I surprised." I can recall only one other instance of a man giving me that look and years later, when I had the opportunity (and no longer feared exposure) to ask him if he had known I was gay and how much import I placed on his look that one day, he had no idea what I was talking about, neither remembering the day or the look or even considering that I was not one or the other.

And is that not what makes the secret of being gay so dangerous? The irrational fear of being discovered, of being found out, of being labeled flawed in some way (it is what many of us were taught, after all) when, at least as concerns the author, no one but yourself is concerned about who you love. That irrational fear works against your better self, hollowing out your insides, leaving all that remains a brittle shell prone to Humpty-Dumpty syndrome (all the king's horses and all the king's men, especially the men, are nothing but your fantasy life).

Freedom is always a surprise. The rebel fighters storm your last defenses and you raise your flag or your flag raises you. A year later I found myself the day after my arrival in Chicago standing in the doorway of a basement apartment on LaSalle Street and Maple on a hot late August afternoon, drying my hair with a towel, a pair of cut-off Levis my modesty panel, otherwise naked, tan, young, golden, and soon cruised and fellated in the dark stairwell, all of it a revelation and a liberation. And left me ready to do it again the very moment it ended.

The Devil and the Details

I guess I could blame the beaten-down, ratty, red hide-a-bed I bought on the cheap from a second-hand store days later that fall in 1973 for what happened. The mattress was thin and lumpy and didn't quite fit the spring system and because I'm extra tall I could hook my toes into the springs at one end and my hands at the other—should there ever be an occasion to do so. The cold steel rail that hoisted and folded the bed back into its couch-shape, which during its first few months of use hardly ever happened. The hide-a-bed, with its bony armature, caught me whenever I needed to get out of bed fast—which was most mornings as I rushed to throw myself together and get to school by the 7:30 call, it's icy scratch against my bare ass a reminder of its low standards.

It's possible that some of my fellow students at the Goodman came home with me before we went out for the evening, to rehearse a scene or run lines; I'm pretty sure I made out with one of the girls in my class on the hide-a-bed, but that evening did not get beyond a lot of fondling and masturbating after she had left. And I know for sure that until May of the following year, no boys/men and I took a tumble on that skimpy little piece of foam with its worn-out blue-striped ticking. Coming home after 12 hours at school, it would welcome me with its un-made-ness, the top sheet pushed to the bottom of the bed where I had kicked it off that morning, the bottom sheet coming untucked at the top and sides, a pillow mashed into a ball pushed up against the back of the sofa and its gleaming undercarriage, like braces on a pubescent teenager, grinning at me. And I'd flop down onto it, its springs singing and laughing at my immaturity and my virginity as it hummed and caressed me, a memory of its better days (were there any?).

The Exorcism

Richard looked at me with his little fox face, black stubble outlining his jaw as he pursed his lips (kiss me, they said) while I leaned into his waiting, open mouth and delivered a blast of weed in a perfect shotgun. The smoke traveled directly down his windpipe, filling his lungs (was that his chest expanding?). His black eyes stared at me truth-or-dare-style, our lips so close that passersby may have mistaken our illicit closeness for lovers slowly dissolving into each other. We were standing in an alley outside of the Chicago Theater on a cool spring night waiting for the next showing of The Exorcist, trying hard not to touch each other. The swirl of lights and noise of honking cars in downtown Chicago was the blurry background to our story (it's true that I remember the pavement slick with a recent spring shower, a mirror held up to the city, reflecting lives and machines in equal parts.)

How did he end up living with me in that tiny little studio, both of us sleeping on the red hide-a-bed? It seemed to me at the time, as it does today, that he was just there one evening, sitting on the unmade bed, his suitcase with all of his worldly goods stuffed inside still in the hallway where he'd dropped it, his wiry frame not unlike the undercarriage of the bed (springy and spare, perhaps a bit dangerous and cold to the touch) and those eyes of his (insert your favorite trite adjective here—deep pools of black, dark stars, sparkling orbs) focused on mine. It would be a temporary arrangement until he got his feet underneath him, he'd just arrived in Chicago from one of the many small towns on the prairies to the west, as so many of us did. He'd been hired to work at the same restaurant I did, cash tips from his last shift tucked into a shirt pocket.

That first night sharing my tiny apartment was a dance of miscues. I thought he wanted me, I know I wanted him; he pushed my advances away that evening under the covers, but hours later when I woke up in the early morning to prepare for school, I felt his erection pressing against my back, a dark-haired forearm holding onto my chest, his fingers lightly grazing a nipple. His little snores seemed like love talk to me as I slipped away from his silent invitation (he'd said, "no" once, who was I to object?), the hide-a-bed doing its best to wake him with my movement out and away from his feral hardness. I tiptoed to the bathroom and then out the door to face the day ahead and although the sun was shining, my head was fogged in with all these yeses and nos rubbing up against each other, a morass of unexplained emotions.

This silly dance of push-me/pull-you continued over the weeks that he spent living with me. I would leave for school in the early morning, home again in the late afternoon where I'd find him taking a bath, hello-ing at me as I walked past the open bathroom door, him slick like an otter , as if my need for him meant nothing, just one more fool following him. I tried to distance myself from him, but in those few square feet of living space, his suitcase closet opened at the foot of the bed; our working together, going out for a drink afterward, stumbling home, falling into the cool embrace of the hide-a-bed, asleep in seconds—arms, legs, warm breath all mixed together.

"Let's go see The Exorcist," he said, "It'll be fun." And because I wanted him to like me enough so that when we slept together it would be more than sleeping, it would be sex, I said, "Sure, let's do it." The marijuana we smoked in the alley wasn't helping make this a pleasurable experience; faces of the other movie-goers kept swimming in and out of my line of vision, everything in slow-/fast motion, a bit of the undersea effect, schools of fish. There just seemed to be so many people all of a sudden. I'd lost sight of Richard in the crowd, the smells of popcorn and that horrible oil they poured over it, a psychedelic swirl of sensory overload and when I did finally settle in a seat next to him, I remember thinking that perhaps I'd never lost sight of him after all. I loathed the film, with its grainy overlay of fear, the priest, the mother, the dirt, the vomit (who the fuck would believe someone's head would spin like that I thought as I grabbed onto to Richard's arm for some comfort— none given— at the spectacle and the crowded theater filled with derisive laughter, chatter, yelling at the screen in encouragement.) "Were they even human?" I asked myself and I turned to look at Richard's foxy profile—the fine line of his nose, those red lips pulled back in a grinning smile at the nonsense on the screen and in the theater then I realized I was wrong about him, that my feelings were wrong, it was all wrong—my revelation underscored by the green slime issuing from poor Linda Blair's mouth.

We walked home from downtown, pausing perhaps for a moment to watch the Chicago River flow backwards, Goldberg's Marina City corn cob towers reflected in the water below the bridge. I don't know if we talked about the movie or if we dished the latest bit of dirt at the restaurant, I don't know what happened right then, but a few days later Richard moved out, a farewell note on the red hide-a-bed with his share of the rent, $50.00. Gone. Vanished. He'd quit the restaurant, disappeared, vamoosed, adios amigo, vaporized, a cloud, a dream, sunshine and moonlight appearing at the same time, me sitting on the bed leaning against the back of it with the pillow he had used held up to my nose, his earthy, earthly scent his good-bye.

Cold

Amish Country

JAMES SCHWARTZ

My father had poor circulation
In his feet which is why
He always wore his socks to bed
Even on August evenings
I inherited this so at least
He left me something
Other than his homophobia
His raised voice, his Amish anger,
Goddamn fuck Daddy,
I'm so bored in the Midwestern matrix,
I always was, I think,
I wear my socks to bed,
Even during sex with the men,
I picked up at bars you don't know,
Do you want to take your socks off?
I do not but if you rip them off me,
I'll feel something more than cold.

Coming Out

St. Louis, MO

ALYSON THOMPSON

My coming out has meant
Coming into myself more fully
Taking up space within myself
Occupying my body as my own
Knowing the sound of my voice
Letting it lead me home

Allowing all that was suppressed
within me to emerge
Allowing all that was silenced
within me to speak
Allowing all that was gestating
within me to be birthed
Allowing all that was damned
within me to become holy

Welch's and Wine

Pittsburgh, PA

ANGELA PUPINO

For an aspiring pastor, I am very bad at taking communion.

When I take communion, I'm all elbows. After I dip my Body of Christ in the Blood of Christ, I hold the Body of Christ far from my body like scientists do with radioactive lab beakers in movies, free hand cupped beneath to catch any errant drips. Then I try not to drip it on my clothes before I can get it into my mouth. And then there's the taste. I can't get over the taste of bread dipped in wine.

United Methodists, true to their teetotaling roots, dip their Body of Christ in grape juice. It makes communion sweet. Wine, used by Lutherans, makes it somewhat bitter.

The first time I took communion with wine, my body recognized the wrong blood type and rejected it accordingly. I spit half of it out, and it dripped down my shirt. If Pastor Brian in his infinite grace and wisdom noticed, he said nothing.

It was my first service with the Pittsburgh Students Active in Lutheran Ministry (yes, PSALM). Eight or so students sat in a circle around a tiny altar in the upstairs chapel of the Lutheran University Center, a squat, redbrick building located on the borderline between the campuses of Carnegie Mellon University and the University of Pittsburgh. That area of the city's Oakland neighborhood is a commercial district with shops and restaurants catering almost exclusively to university students. Starbucks, cheap Chinese food, and a grill with $5 Moscow mules during happy hour. Years earlier the Lutheran University Center was remodeled into a more welcoming space, and it needed to compete architecturally with the sleek Jewish University Center down the street. Before that, I am told, it was a bomb shelter.

They did an admirable job of making the place feel spiritual with artistic displays. Among the stacks of worn books and chairs: A tiny stained-glass Lutheran rose on the window in the corner. A spiraling wooden sculpture hung from the ceiling above the altar. Long candlesticks that glisten in the light. Despite a campus ministry budget, the place felt well loved. A tiny cathedral tucked away in an attic two doors down from a bagel place that also sells milkshakes.

Earlier that night I stopped into the Lutheran University Center for dinner. There's always something unsettling about being the new person in a religious space. Eyes gravitate to you, welcoming and hopeful but also gearing up for conversion. If not conversion to their faith, at least to their particular congregation.

It didn't help that Pastor Brian, who was cooking dinner with a few other students in the kitchen, was half-expecting me. After a few hours spent crying earlier in the week, I sent him a panicked email. "Former (?) United Methodist Student Looking to Connect" was the subject line, and it was as much of a newspaper personals ad as it sounds.

He responded within an hour with an invitation to the group's weekly dinner. And here I was.

Pastor Brian is a fairly tall man, bearded like all male campus ministers seem to be. Later I will find out that he was the Dungeon Master for the students' *Dungeons and Dragons* campaign and ran a Christian podcast about *Game of Thrones*. He's also an amateur photographer and a nearly professional chef.

I managed to squeak out, "I'm Angela." Pastor Brian's face lit up with recognition.

As I helped them set the table and helped myself to dinner, I realized how desperate I had become for a spiritual community. Graduate school is academically strenuous for everyone, but I couldn't get over the feeling that Carnegie Mellon was running an elaborate experiment to see how many classes it could cram into a semester before all the students had breakdowns. Ten? Eleven? No wonder I needed Jesus.

The Lutherans were a ragtag bunch of undergraduate students, largely nerdy, and almost entirely from the University of Pittsburgh. They made *Doctor Who* references over dinner and offered to take me on a tour of their campus.

Awkwardly, I introduced myself to the new, hopeful faces. I'm a graduate student at Carnegie Mellon. Studying Public Policy. Grew up outside of Youngstown.

Then I said, "I was raised United Methodist." That struck a chord.

"Oh," said one of the students, a biology major and religion minor. "They're the ones that were just in the news for keeping gay people out, right?"

Earlier that week the United Methodist Church had voted in a global meeting to reaffirm and strengthen its ban on "self-avowed, practicing homosexuals" in the clergy. A ban on exactly who I aspired to be.

A blush settled onto my cheeks. I also needed a spiritual community because mine was dying.

Vichna Pamyat

In memory of my father, Vyacheslav

Chicago, IL

ANDRIY PARTYKEVICH

I fell in love with the Orthodox Church when I was around 8 years old.

As a family, we did not go to church very often. We were the children of a mixed marriage—mixed religiously and ethnically. It was a great distance from our home in the suburbs to an "acceptable" Orthodox Church in Chicago's "Ukrainian village," one of the right ethnic variety for my father—a father who worked many hours.

My father fought in World War II, fighting for an independent Ukrainian state. He immigrated to the United States where he and numerous other Ukrainians were free to form communities that would keep the Ukrainian language, customs and traditions alive. Because of the Soviet domination of Ukraine, and the Russification of the Soviet Union, the diaspora provided the only hope for a living tradition to survive and even flourish. Aside from youth organizations, cultural clubs and numerous other venues, Ukrainian churches, both Orthodox and Eastern Catholic, were the most numerous and permanent resources for fostering Ukrainian communities and keeping the Ukrainian language alive.

It was the beauty of the Ukrainian Orthodox church that drew me in—the mellifluous and prayerful voice of the elderly archbishop whose name was Hryhoriy, his very careful but deliberate movements, the splendor of the music and chanting coming from the choir loft, and the sight and smell of incense emanating from the altar, which seemed like a wonderful combination of flowers and scrumptious food cooking.

There were also two very important "tastings" at every Liturgy that we attended: the prosphora (antidoron—blessed bread) at the end of the service, and the candy from the purse of my *babtsya*, my grandmother, given to me at some point, usually during the sermon that was almost incomprehensible to me, as it was in Ukrainian.

By that time, as a young teenager, I knew that I was different. I did not yet call myself gay or even a homosexual—but I knew that I was different. Yet my relationship with the Church intensified. Guided by a very loving, kind and caring priest, Father Orest, I became an altar server and reader in the church, chanting the psalms before Liturgy.

When I graduated from high school, I was determined to enter Seminary in order to prepare for the priesthood. My father was cautious, concerned that the life of a priest was difficult. The Ukrainian phrase that he used was that being a priest was "тяжкий хліб" or a "tough piece of bread," but he did give me his blessing to enter the Seminary. Christ had called me to the priesthood, and I began my journey through prayer and study to ordination. Strange now to think that, by then, I knew I was gay, God knew I was gay, but the Church could not or must not. I lived in fear of the authorities of the Church, the Bishop, the Rector of the Seminary, or any influential priest in the archdiocese from finding out that I was gay. I knew that if my secret was discovered, I would be found out, and told to leave Seminary and my dream of becoming a priest would end. In a small, and tight-knit world like the Ukrainian Orthodox community, it was very possible that my secret would leak out to every parishioner at my home parish in Illinois.

Throughout my years of study at Seminary, my father and mother were very proud of me, especially when I was able to return to my home parish in Addison during winter and summer vacations and allowed to preach to the congregation. My father used to prod the local pastor to allow me to preach. The harder conversation with my "*tato*" (father in Ukrainian) came months after graduating from Seminary and telling him that I intended to ask to be ordained as a celibate priest. In the Orthodox Church, priests may choose to be married (to women, of course), but the marriage must take place before ordination.

My father was very worried that I would be alone in my life, and that I would have a very difficult time living as an unmarried man. He believed that everyone needed someone to love and care for in their lives, and was deeply concerned that I would not have someone in my life to love and to be loved by. I tried to convince him that after much prayer, thought and preparation, that this was my true desire. I was fairly certain that he was unconvinced; he nonetheless gave me his blessing to petition the bishop for ordination as an unmarried man. Of course in the pit of my stomach, I knew that the real reason was that I wanted to be a priest with all my heart, but marrying a woman would ruin her life and mine.

I was ordained in 1982. The ordaining Archbishop, Metropolitan Mstyslav, was happy to ordain me during the celebration of the 40th anniversary of his episcopal consecration - quite an honor. An entire busload of parishioners traveled from the parish in Addison to South Bound Brook,

NJ to witness and celebrate my ordination. The following Sunday, I served my first Divine Liturgy in my home parish, which was followed by a banquet in my honor. I was humbled.

Much later, after over twenty years of priestly service—in the parish, teaching at the diocesan Seminary and working closely with the hierarchy of the Church, and nominated several times to be a bishop (which I always declined)—I was thoroughly convinced of my father's love for me, as well as his admiration and respect for my chosen path in life.

What my father did not know was that over those years, his concerns about being alone proved to be true. It was difficult to be alone, to live alone, to not have anyone special in my life to love and care for, someone who loved and cared for me. What my father also did not know was that it would have been impossible for me to have gotten married to a woman. I did not believe that the priesthood would turn me straight, or take away the feelings that I had, but I did spend years hoping, praying, fasting, visiting holy men and traveling to monasteries in New York State and Pennsylvania, with the sincere hope that God would take away my desires and feelings and longing for another man to love and spend my life with. What my father also did not know was that I constantly questioned my calling to the priesthood. Why would God call me, a gay man, to be a priest if He did not also give me the charism—the gift—to live a chaste and celibate life? The turmoil was significant and something I believed I could not share with my father. Why?

When my brothers and I were younger—I was in 6th or 7th grade—I vividly remember my father telling us that if he ever found out that one of us was a "homo", he would kill us. I am not sure what provoked my father, who was not a violent man. He never even hit us as children, but for some reason, he felt compelled to say this to his sons. Did he see something in me? In relating this episode many years later to a dear friend, he questioned the veracity of my memory. How and why would a child ever make something like this up? What child would believe that their parent had within them the possibility to harm their children, especially if all that child knew was love and care from their parents? Of course, I knew that my father would not have ever harmed us, but what I do know is that for decades I lived with the fear that one day he would find out that I was gay. And in my mind, I was certain that that meant losing my father's love and respect.

The Creator, in His unfathomable wisdom, created me as a gay man. Christ, the High Priest, called me, a gay man, to be a priest in His church. He did not ask me to renounce my sexuality, the sexuality that He gave me, nor did He call me to be celibate. This is the beauty of the diversity of creation from the same Lord who gave us the beauty of the Orthodox Church that I became enamored with as a child. Only years later did I realize that the institutional church demanded that I hide and remain silent about the true person that God had made.

I left the active priesthood in 2002. Two summers before, I traveled to the Holy Mountain of Athos in Greece to ask God, for the final time, to take away the desires. While in Greece, God led me to a small cafe where I would meet my future husband. Following more prayer and discernment, I informed the bishop that I was leaving the parish and would not seek an additional assignment.

For years, my father wondered why I no longer served in the Church. It was a topic that I refused to discuss with him. My father died never fully knowing the full truth about his son. He never had the pleasure of meeting the most wonderful man who changed my life, who is now my husband. Frequently I ask myself and search my conscience for regrets of not sharing with my father what he surely already knew. I wonder why I was afraid, and why I was such a coward. And now I must live with the thought that I will never be able to share my truth with my father and that I might always live with those regrets. Certainly, it was not because I believe I made the wrong choice to leave the active priesthood, or marry the man I love. It was the fear of losing my father's love. To be truthful, I never gave him the choice to accept or reject me, and that I regret.

Many of us have regrets in our life, for things that we should have said or done, and for times when we should have kept silent or not acted. We agonize about being candid and telling our truth, especially to those we love and from whom we crave respect. LGBT Orthodox Christians especially worry about telling their spiritual fathers that they were created differently, although very much in the image of our Creator. Called to be honest, we are particularly troubled that our families would not understand us, would lack compassion, would condemn us, or even bar us from the family, including the family of Christ within the Church. No child of God should ever wonder if they are loved or will be loved.

The strange thing about the truth is that no matter how hard you try to hide it—it remains the truth—even when unspoken—it is revealed.

Forgive me, Dad.
Memory Eternal, Dad.   Vichna Pamyat, Tato.

Pillar

Peoria, IL

CARMEN SMITH

I look back at what was my home.
They called down God's fire upon it
so I can't return. They say I
am the cause of its burning.

It does not matter, the ravaging,
the chaos, the daughters offered, expendable.
It does not matter, the neighbors turned mob,
the bartering of lives, the ashes of God's spit
on His creation, the fire rain of a justice
that drives people from their homes
and demands they not even look back.

No.

Somewhere is a god that is ocean salt,
a god that is the daughters, the wife grieving
over a lost home.

The Inexperience

I-55

JESSIE KEARY

Corporeal forms are OUT.

The word "woman" makes my skin crawl,
makes me aware of skin.

I have no leg(s) to stand on.

I hover above a crumpled heap of me.

I am the Holy Spirit, a tongue of flame.

I whisper every language as one, but
can't say my own name.

Where the light enters

Lac du Flambeau Reservation, WI

KAI MINOSH PYLE

they call it waswaaganing—lac du flambeau—lake of the flaming torches. all fish eye reflections and fading sunset and pinprick stars. balancing on the canoe's edge, i see myself looking into the water for that tell-tale light. hand trembling with the weight of burning birch bark.

an ancient sturgeon swims up to the side of the boat and looks me right in the eye. it knows i'm not here for the fish. it knows the size of the black hole inside me. the one that devours the light. the sturgeon stands up in the water and becomes a man. it reaches out and takes the torch from me so gently. i am still teetering in the canoe when it cradles my head and touches burning spruce gum to my skin.

screaming, i don't move. the light is brighter than anything i've ever seen. cauterizing before my own eyes.

"you learn," the sturgeon says, "to live with it."

The Son

Scaly Mountain, NC

JEFFERY BEAM

When the moon
whitens the deer
and sweet doves
croon
against the plow

with a deer's light
footsteps I'll creep
next to the hunter's
fire.
The son

they forgot.
Who, too,
knows how to fire
a primal urge.
Who, too,

from the coral woods
by the camp fire dances
into
the circular
light.

Jeffery Beam © 2012, *The New Beautiful Tendons: Collected Queer Poems 1969-2012*, Triton-Spuyten/Duyvil

Kindergarten

Cicero, IL

JOSÉ QUIÑONES

The living room was dark and quiet; the rain that was crashing into the window had subsided to nothingness as the straggling drops were finding their way down the window. Chicago is known for having multiple seasons in one day, but today it simply stuck with spring showers and fall breezes. The leaves were a crisp yellow and orange, being swept from their branches by the cool breeze, piling on each other once they hit the ground, ending their cycle. The ambiance in the living room was dull, the usual when a storm passes by. I was sitting alone, trying to charge my iPod, so that I could go walk around the city—my go-to when I wanted to clear my mind. My mother was in the kitchen making food. The smell of boiling corn seeping into my nose. She had the tv on and I could hear the hostesses from Primer Impacto giving their news story, her go-to background noise when she wanted to concentrate on making food.

My mother is a very religious woman, and you can tell when looking around the living room. There are portraits of saints she holds true patronage to. Crosses are scattered throughout. When I was younger, I was as religious as her—some of the images around the house are ones that I won for her at festivals in her hometown in Mexico. Every saint she has collected, she made into a shrine in her bedroom, all featured behind a Bible my dad bought. I like to remember how when we watched telenovelas, she would switch the channel if two men, or women, were making out with each other. At an early age, I knew what was wrong and what was right, in the eyes of God, who watched everything we did and would judge us to hell or accept us into heaven. I knew stealing was wrong, I knew lying was bad, and I knew homosexuality was not accepted.

Our living room was filled with plants that my mother nurtured. She was born to be a mother. Everything she took care of blossomed.

"Tienes hambre?" she called from the kitchen.

"No gracias," I responded. "En un rato me voy a ir a caminar al centro."

She continued to cook, and I continued to wait for my iPod. I looked out the window and saw that there were no more raindrops, but only the wind disheveling the trees around our house.

The first time I ever kissed a boy was in kindergarten. The memory is vivid, and it often crosses my mind. We were sitting on the floor, being read to; all of our eager eyes wanting to know what was going to come next. The room was decorated with the alphabet, pictures of the changing seasons, and booming with every color under the rainbow—it was a place of discovery. I was sitting next to the boy I felt some strange attraction to; his face was looking at Ms. Morales, our kindergarten teacher. There was something about it, but I knew that this feeling wasn't supposed to feel normal. I couldn't stop staring, though, and the more I stared, the more I felt myself gravitating towards him. As the class continued to listen attentively to Ms. Morales, I looked around to see if anyone was looking at me. When no one was, I leaned over and kissed him on the cheek. I immediately turned back to Ms. Morales and pretended nothing had happened. But something had happened. I felt an oncoming sensation of happiness.

"Porque siempre vas a caminar al centro?" I turned towards the kitchen, and my mother was looking at me as she asked.

"No lo sé, me gusta para no pensar tanto en las cosas" I turned back towards looking outside.

The first person I made out with was the summer after my junior year. I had been hired at the pool in our neighboring town, and he was the head guard. On our very last day of working at the pool, he told me he needed some help in the heater room, so I naively followed. He closed the door behind him, grabbed me, and pressed me up against the wall, "I've been waiting for this moment." Those words took me by surprise, but also brought back the sensation of happiness I had not felt since kindergarten. We continued to hang out days after that, but we never got to fully experience one-another. It was a summer fling that lasted well into my senior year but remained a fling.

I looked at the family picture of my parents and I that was in our tv stand. My dad wore his signature mustache and sported a khaki coat with a crisp white shirt and a blue and red striped tie. My mother wore her hair up—the higher the hair, the closer to God. She had on a blue nautical dress—the most beautiful woman I ever laid my eyes on. I was about three and I had a pout on my face, and I accessorized it with a navy suit and a red tie. The frame has 'I Love My Daddy' written around it; our perfect little family of three. Yet, I knew that when they find out that I was gay, that would change everything; it would change how they looked at their pride and joy, and that was something that I wasn't willing to risk, because I loved them so much.

The TV from the kitchen goes silent and I look down at my iPod to see it is finally charged. I start gathering my stuff and go to get my jacket when my mom comes into the living room and sits down on a chair. When I get back from getting my jacket, she's still sitting there looking outside the same window I was looking at, entranced. "Siéntate," she tells me. I sit.

My mother is one of 14 children. She is the third oldest child and the oldest daughter. My grandfather was a farmer and my grandmother sewed tablecloths and did other projects. Since my mother was the oldest daughter, she was tasked with helping my grandmother care for her younger siblings. As more of my aunts and uncles came into this world, my mother took care of them as her own; she never went to school and never learned to read or write properly, but that didn't stop her. When she was older, and the majority of her siblings were old enough to go to school in Mexico, she would help my grandmother with all the housework and also began sewing with her. As my aunts and uncles got older, they began to emigrate to the United States. My mother took this as her chance to explore the world she couldn't in school. They all settled in Chicago and began working, while my mother would often care for their children. She met my dad through my aunt's husband, and she likes to tell me that she hated him at first, because their first date was to a circus and he ate all the popcorn. Several months later, they would have me. Their shame and disgust, yearning to be their pride and joy.

I sit across from her and look at the clock because I know I'm going to be late getting to the city. When I look back at her, she is looking at me. "Qué pasó, ama?" I ask her.

"Yo sé," she says.

I was confused. I didn't know what she was talking about. "Usted sabe qué?"

"Yo sé que eres gay," she tells me.

I look back at the clock and it seems like I forgot what I was trying to find. I was trying to avoid making eye contact with her, because I didn't want her to know that I was guilty of it all. I didn't want to see the shame in her face. "Siempre he sabido que eras gay," she says.

I look up and see that she's sitting next to me. I tell her, "La quiero, ama."

"Yo también te quiero, mijo." We hug.

Don't Rain on My Parade

Ralston, NE

ZACH BENAK

Judy Morrison outed me when I was five-years-old. As a Kindergarten teacher over two decades into her career, she was adept at observing problematic behaviors in children, and disciplining them as she saw fit. In 2002, I was the child being brought to a heel, as she noted my playground habits as cause for parental concern.

"Zach only plays with girls," Mrs. Morrison told my mom at my first parent-teacher conference. And in that moment, a woman who dressed like a gay icon, with gaudy floral patterns and bulky-buttoned sweater vests, was instead a gay opponent, exposing queer behavior that was especially abnormal for a boy at St. Gerald Catholic School in suburban Nebraska.

But Mrs. Morrison was telling the truth. I spent every recess in Kindergarten with my best friend, Claire, where we would pretend to be spies and peel paint off of a red basketball pole. I had playdates with other girls, where I was allowed to try on cheap lace dresses and chiffon scarves under the guise of playing "Dress Up." I had no interest in flag football, and the only reason I played soccer was for the fun costume: neon shin guards and maroon knee-high socks. Perpetually short and incessantly scrawny, I always lacked the physicality needed for sports and roughhousing. I much preferred to think or talk, especially when it came to all things pop culture and celebrity.

Somewhere between Kindergarten and second grade, around the same age that I was giggling with girls on the swing sets, I got in the habit of checking the mail every day, looking forward to the biweekly arrival of my mom's *People Magazine* subscription. When I was at home during the summer, my trips across the street to the mailbox came multiple times a day, eagerness running high as I waited for the next magazine issue to arrive. I'd march across the street in my suburban neighborhood, wave to the retirees mowing their emerald lawns, and stick my toes in the warm, squishy tar that filled the road's cracks and became gooey under the dry sun. I'd complete this ritual by opening our rusting black mailbox, hoping to find Julia Roberts' glossy face wedged between our cable bills. When the magazine did come, I would pore over its contents, reading up on Brangelina's latest adoptions, or the death of Anna Nicole Smith. I loved my glimpse glimpsing into the lives of these beautiful people, and learning about life's most dramatic occurrences, like affairs and suicides and drug overdoses.

My love for celebrities like Sandra Bullock and Halle Berry reflected my fascination with all things femme. Oscar Red Carpets and glamorous photo shoots hinted at the many secrets lurking behind femininity, sparking my boyhood interest in girlhood. What was the difference between a skirt and a skort? What intricate processes were required for braiding hair—something I couldn't achieve with my blonde bowl cut? And what *did* girls do at sleepovers? These questions didn't stem from curiosity regarding the opposite sex—they came from jealousy. I felt excluded from the feminine narrative that I wanted to be a part of, and my revolutionary and entirely unintentional efforts to break down these barriers resulted in negative criticism, and not just from Mrs. Morrison.

"I don't remember how I felt, so I must not have cared," my mom texted me recently, after I asked her about Mrs. Morrison's remark. "But I do remember you being the only boy invited to some girl's birthday party, and listening to one mom go on and on about you only playing with girls, and I did not like her implications." I pictured my mother enjoying a late summer breeze on the back deck of the same home that I grew up in, slowly typing on her phone, furrowing her eyebrow behind her thin black bifocals, and recalling the speculation and commentary she endured within the Midwestern Catholic community that we had both distanced ourselves from in recent years. What was it really like for her, being the mother of a boy who was always unlike others?

"I never liked those women, anyway," my mom concluded, instinctually defensive of her son, then and now.

A version of "Don't Rain on my Parade" originally appeared in the Paragon Press.

dalkaygii

St. Louis, MO

YASMIN BASHIR

I fear that when you die
I will forget what home is.
that my spirit will be too weak
to retell your stories.

but i must remember
that you have left us
with a map.
engraved onto each
of our bodies
Is a reminder of what home is.

adorned on my arms
is tracings of
the warm berbera river.
this water holds stories told by
everyone that has
walked alongside it;
we will go there to heal.

our skin is stained with
the complexion of each of our ancestors.
when we feel words of poison,
we will look down
at our amber hands.
this is here to remind
us that there is a land
where our bodies are loved.

close your eyes
imagine that land

you will see rows of women
draped in printed sheets
lined up to hold you
in their arms.
they will kiss your face and say:

"waxaad leedahay indhaheeda" "you have your mother's eyes"
"iyo maqaarkeda" "and her skin"

Nine Forms of the Goddess

Cross Lanes, WV

NEEMA AVASHIA

It is 1982, and nine Indian women gather in a circle in a basement in Cross Lanes, West Virginia to celebrate the festival of Navratri. The basement floor is covered with bright blue carpet, the walls lined with brown, faux-wood paneling, and there is a red metal beam in the center of the room where a lighted brass pot called a *garbo* and idols of deities typically stand. Women, in sharp contrast to their damp surroundings, who are dressed in their heaviest silk saris and best jewelry: finery brought with them in suitcases that travelled 8,000 miles from India to New York, sometimes by way of Africa or London, and then another 500 from Queens to the Appalachian hills of West Virginia.

They are strangers in the strangest of lands, brought to the capital city of Charleston by engineer and doctor husbands who service the coal and chemical industries. The women spend the majority of their time in white, largely working-class spaces, trying to bridge the divide between their Indian accents and their neighbors' Southern ones, their Hindu culture and the Bible Belt. Only on weekends and holidays do they find the opportunity to connect with others who share the same language, faith, and customs. A brief respite from a steady sensation of foreignness that pervades their day-to-day.

Each autumn, the women gather for nine nights, or as many as they can spare. Each night, a different color inspires their clothing. Each night, a different incarnation of the goddess Durga is the focus of their worship. Durga, queen among Hindu goddesses, warrior for good, vanquisher of evil. She is often depicted astride a tiger, holding a sword, a trident, a mace, and a dagger in her many hands. *Durga* literally means unassailable. She is the Mother goddess who will not be challenged or questioned in her battle to preserve the dharma of the righteous.

These worshippers of Durga begin each night the same way, singing the *mataji na garba* in voices that are pitched and clear. With their words, they praise the many forms and powers of the Mother goddess. They slowly clap and slide around the circle, their motions repetitive and rhythmic. They pick up speed. The two-clap step builds to three. Their bodies blur, faces lost in a whirl of spinning, shining colors. The smell of sweat, mixing with perfume and powder, fills the room. In the morning, tiny purple bruises will dot their arms, induced by the repeated banging of their glass bangles. The soles of their feet will bear the red flames of carpet burn. Their waists will host a near-permanent indentation from the tightness of their petticoats. But for these nine nights, there is no pain insufferable enough to make them leave the circle early.

This is the festival of Navratri. In Gujarati, *Nav* means nine, and *rat* means night. Nine women, nine nights, nine colors. Nine forms of the Mother goddess spinning in front of me.

More than 35 years later, I live in Boston, Massachusetts, one of the oldest cities in the U.S.; home to Harvard and MIT and several other distinguished universities. Despite its five million people, I have no Indian community to speak of. There are weekend Navratri garbas in the suburbs, massive gatherings of Indians I do not know, in the gymnasiums of middle schools I've never heard of. I feel no pull to go to these anonymous celebrations where ritual feels meaningless in the absence of relationships. Instead, the sharpest pang is the one asking me to go backwards in time, back to the tiny Indian community nestled in the Kanawha Valley, back to the basement in Cross Lanes, back to the garba where the faces in the circle are the faces of my many mothers, and their characters are the unassailable personifications of *Navadurga*.

Though I was just three at the time, when I envision the Cross Lanes garba, I see myself as I look now, and my mothers are all my age. I take the place of *Shailaputri*, worshipped on the first day of Navratri. Like her, I, too, am a daughter of the mountains. Born and raised in West Virginia, I straddle the culture of my parents and the culture of my Appalachian birthplace. Autumn elicits nostalgia not just for Navratri but also for the mountains of my home state, set aflame in oranges, yellows, and reds. I experience a double-loss each Fall, missing both the mountains of my childhood and the many mothers who played a role in raising me there. In Gujarati, the word for maternal aunt is *ma-si*—"mother-like". So to my mother's chosen sisters I cleaved. Because of the familiarity they provided in the most foreign of contexts, they became my *masis*. My mother-likes.

As the lone Indian girl in my classes at school, I was surrounded by white girls whose parents allowed them to dress in tight clothing, wear make-up, and put chemicals in their hair. Whether because of my awkward appearance, my brown skin, my yet-to-be-realized sexuality, or some combination of the three, dating was never an option for me. I knew that I could not be like the girls in my classes, but struggled to find a cohesive identity for myself.

So it came to be that my many mothers took the traditional place of aunts and cousins in teaching me how to be a good woman, and how to live a righteous life. In the absence of any other role models to help me understand what it meant to be an Indian woman, and what it meant to be in a relationship, their definitions are the ones I used to construct my own identity—sometimes by reflecting their image, and sometimes in direct opposition to it.

Dancing beside me in this ring of women is Indira auntie, the mother of my oldest childhood friend. She embodies *Bhramacharini*, the incarnation of Durga best known for her devout austerity. For the entirety of my childhood Indira auntie lived in a one-level, 3-bedroom house with her husband and five children; on a single income earned at a low-paying job in the West Virginia state government.

I invaded her house and refrigerator on a regular basis, sleeping over for multiple nights at a time, and consuming every pickle in every jar, draining them of their neon brine afterwards. In retrospect, I can recognize the very real financial struggles that her family faced. The ramen noodle lunches that felt like a guilty pleasure to me when compared with my doctor-dad's demands that we eat fiber and salad were a necessary staple in her feeding five growing children. Yet never once did she make me feel as though I was draining her wallet, or that there wasn't room for me at her brown laminate dining table.

Indira auntie's house was the first place where I remember having conscious questions about gender in Indian culture. Auntie had four daughters, and one son. Yet their car's license plate carried their son's name. So did the family business, even though her daughters were the ones earning honor roll, becoming valedictorians, and getting full scholarships to college. I never got the sense this was auntie's choice. But what did it mean about an Indian woman's ability to recognize and reward her daughters? To value and honor the lives they were creating, instead of simply valuing a son for his male-ness?

As I watched Indira auntie's daughters rack up their awards, I wondered: what level of accomplishment would a woman need to ascend to in order for her success to outweigh her gender?

On the other side in the nine-woman circle stands Asha auntie, exuding the peace and tranquility of *Chandraghanta*. A pale-skinned Punjabi, with angular features and the most lilting of all the auntie's accents, Asha auntie showed her love for us through her cooking. I have never tasted a paneer dish in a restaurant, or in another home, that comes anywhere close to the perfect texture and seasoning of food I ate in her kitchen.

Even when I was young, I was cognizant of Asha auntie's grace and femininity—her perfectly coiffed hair, manicured nails, and beautifully tailored suits. Being around her heightened my awareness of my own frizzy hair, dark skin, bitten down nails and baggy clothes. I did not want to be like her; I simply saw in her a kind of womanhood that I was certain I could never approximate.

What's more, she navigated the painful economic divide between her and her wealthier friends with a kind of grace that blew me away as I got older and could see the strain it placed on their relationships. While her friends bought increasingly bigger houses and fancier cars, Asha auntie's living conditions stayed the same. My mom used to say that you could show up at Asha auntie's door at any time, on any day, and never feel anything but welcome. Unemployment, caring for aging parents, financial hardship—the weight of it all never showed on her face.

Asha auntie, who worked the hardest, also died the youngest, of a lung cancer whose source we never understood. It was my many mothers who washed her body, combed her hair, trimmed her nails, did her make-up, and wrapped her in a sari for the final time before her cremation.

Across the circle is the eldest of my mothers, and the elder in our community, Shobana auntie. She was one of the first Indians to come to the Kanawha Valley in the mid 60s, forging the path for the hundred or so families who would eventually come to live in our community. Her husband, Sharad uncle, was killed in a terrible accident when his car was sideswiped as he pulled onto Big Tyler Road. Their children were barely teenagers at the time.

After his death, Shobana auntie became our community's first single mother, the living embodiment of *Kushmanda*, the deity who represents strength and courage in the face of adversity. She invited me to her house high on the hill of Mourning Dove for *thalipit*, a traditional Maharastrian dish, every time I came home from college. And no matter how badly her arthritic hands ached, or how hard her fingers fought against yielding to their clenched-fist state, she refused to let me help her pat the dough into shape, or fry it on the skillet.

"You sit and rest," she would say. "You work so hard in school. The least I can do is feed you."

In a culture where the quantity of *ghee* used is equated with the quantity of love felt, Shobana auntie's *thalipit* always arrived at the table with innumerable pools of clarified butter glistening on its crispy surface.

Shobhana auntie's neighbor, both in the circle and in our town of Cross Lanes, is Jyoti auntie. Her enthusiasm for garba, and the grace with which she moves around the *garbo*, is unmatched. The shortest of all the women, with a braid that runs half the length of her body, she makes up in energy what she lacks in height. She is *Skanda Mata* incarnate—pure and divine of nature. The most religiously devout of my mothers, Jyoti auntie is the person to ask when questions of ritual or faith arise. She is also a walking Gujarati dictionary, and the sunniest person I know.

When I took my white, Jewish/Irish/Italian female partner to West Virginia to meet my mothers, and sent a hesitant text to each one asking if they wanted to meet us, this was the rejoinder that she and her husband Praful uncle sent:

Neema, I am angry with you that you felt the need to call and ask if we are ok with your and Laura's visit. We are your second home and family. So no matter what, we will always be there for you. Also don't waste your money by staying in a hotel or some other place. We have plenty of rooms (may not be as clean) and save money for the gas (went up yesterday by 40 cents per gallon). See you soon.

Their words were cathartic, followed by actions that further confirmed a fact I should have known all along—that for my mothers, love dampened any prejudices that might have occurred to them otherwise.

Jyoti auntie embraced Laura, and called her *beta* (my child), as she did for all of the young people in our community. After meeting us in a restaurant for dinner, she insisted that we come to her house and sit in her living room, where she plied us with slices of mango pie and cups of chai. There was no judgement in her heart, only a kind of unconditional love and acceptance that I am blessed to have bestowed upon me.

The owner of the basement where this garba unfolded, Ranju auntie, makes her way around the circle beside Jyoti auntie. She is a living mani-festation of *Katyayani*, who is described as having wild hair and 18 arms, and emitting a radiant light from her body which makes it impossible for darkness and evil to hide. Ranju auntie is tall, with untamed curly hair and a Cindy Crawford mole above her lip, and by far the most disciplinarian of my mothers.

I simultaneously feared Ranju auntie, and was awed by her. Her magical sitting room, with its zebra skin wall hangings, orange plush birdcage chair, and cinema organ, was so different from the staid furniture in my own house, and in those of my neighbors. Her kitchen almost always had a caged bird in it that would utter random Gujarati phrases when you walked in.

Once, my parents left me in her care when they went out of town. During our time together, she decided to take me to Sears for a photoshoot. Ranju auntie styled my long, curly hair in a fashion far different from my traditional braid. She dressed me in cute jeans, a fitted red Sesame Street turtleneck, and cowboy boots, and coaxed me into a pose where I am sitting with one leg crossed over the other, laughing almost flirtatiously.

It is the most "girly" photo in my album of pictures from childhood—somehow managing to be more feminine than all of my awkward prom pictures combined. She didn't ask my parents for permission to take these photos beforehand, just gave them the prints afterwards. Proof, perhaps, that my tomboy self could be tamed if they took it upon themselves to do the taming, as she had.

Ranju auntie lost her pain-filled battle with oral cancer before I could ask her the questions I now have about her childhood in Tanzania, about being a working mom when so many of her peers were staying at home, about being unafraid to live her life in the boldest of reds, greens, and yellows even as those around her continually tried to tone her down.

Next to Ranju auntie is my mother's best friend in this group, Shobha auntie. Her garba style is more stiff and mechanical than that of her neighbors in the circle. Garba is not Shobha auntie's strong suit, in the way that it is for some of the other women, but she participates nonetheless. The mother of three sons, Shobha auntie has called my sister and me her daughters from the outset. We benefit from all of her motherly love, with none of the filial responsibility.

She fills yoghurt containers with enough fried snacks to last me for weeks after a visit, insists that I eat a meal with her at her home high in the hills that ring the city of Charleston, and cooks my favorite foods, most especially her okra, which is crispy in a way I am never able to replicate. Shobha auntie was the first person my mom called when I came out to her, and she embraced Laura with the no-nonsense logic that she applies to all situations.

"If Neema is happy, and Laura makes her happy, that is what matters to me," she told my mom. Whenever my mom has struggled with reconciling my identity with the beliefs of her traditional Indian family, it is Shobha auntie who has counseled her, firmly stating that those family members need to "figure it out and deal with it," and that it isn't my job, or my mom's, to accommodate them.

Though she has always been consistent with me, Shobha auntie's personality is much like that of *Kaal Ratri*, the goddess who is both honored and feared. She runs hot and cold in a way that can leave her friends feeling abandoned at times. I watched my mom's friendship with Shobha auntie ebb and flow over the years, and learned from their interactions how to navigate the changing terrain of friendship, how to provide space without running away.

To Shobha auntie's right in the circle, my sister Swati dances with abandon, her heavy sari no match for her love of dancing. Her eyes are bright and lined with kohl, her long black hair spills down her back. Born when my mother was just 21, and seven years older than me, Swati has always inhabited a strange space in our family—closer to a sister than daughter for my mom, and closer to a mother than sister for me.

Swati is the voice of calm and reason in this group, the goddess *Maha Gauri*, whose primary power is her ability to allay fears. When I decided to start telling my family about Laura—the only relationship I've ever shared with them—there was no doubt in my mind that Swati was the person to confide in first.

I called her one summer evening in 2010 from the parking lot of Roxbury Community College in Boston, where I was attending a teacher training. Words spilled out in a rush, some combination of, "I'm dating a woman," "It's serious," and "Please don't tell mom and dad yet."

There was no hesitation in Swati's voice when she finally got a chance to speak. "I'm so happy for you, Neema. I can't wait to meet her."

It was Swati who coached me through how to tell my mom about Laura. It is Swati who has held every debrief conversation with my mom when she hasn't understood my choices: Why, for example, I won't attend a wedding when Laura's name isn't written on the invitation. Or why I don't want to visit India after hearing homophobic comments from family members on my last visit.

And it is Swati who now helps me navigate new terrain: that of trying to become a mother myself, in a way that none of my many mothers was able to model for me.

The last person in this tight circle of fabric and flesh is my own mother, her smiling face ringed by wisps of hair that have escaped from her tight braid. She is the one whose singing voice I hear most clearly, because it is the voice that never falters during garba. Her grace and femininity are traits I have come to appreciate over the years, even as I've come to accept that they have been passed on to my sister and niece, while skipping over me. Acceptance of this fact has not come as easily for her.

When I was small, my mom sang the same bedtime songs to me that her older brother had sung to her when she was growing up. One, in particular, stands out in my mind. It was a song about a single woman who doesn't understand why she is still single. Each verse outlines all of the qualities that make her a desirable bride. Her father has a car, her grandfather has a horse and buggy, her uncle has a flower garden. She is fairer than her older sister, and skinnier than her younger sister. She goes to college, goes out to eat in restaurants, and goes to see movies. And yet, despite all of this, she remains single.

My mom took the song's message at face-value: the role of a woman in India was to marry, bear children, and be an obedient wife and giving mother. She performed those gendered expectations to the best of her ability. I listened to the same song and thought, in the words of any typical 6-year old, "What kind of capitalist, sexist, shadist nonsense is this?" Our paths in life have been quite different as a result. She has been married to my father for almost 50 years while I have been in a same-sex relationship with my partner, Laura, for the last nine without any ceremony conferring it legal status.

In this group of women, my mother is the peacemaker and the relationship-builder. When she moved away from the Kanawha Valley after thirty years of living there, the ties among the rest of the women slowly unraveled. My mother is *Siddhidatri*, the giver of supernatural powers. She constantly seeks out learning opportunities and ways to share her experiences with those around her. More than any of her peers, she threw herself into the broader American community of Charleston, West Virginia. She did taxes for free at the local library for the working class white folks who needed help completing their paperwork. She volunteered as a docent in our tiny art museum. She became the leader of my Girl Scout troop and used the opportunity to educate my white peers about Indian culture and customs. She earned her MBA at night, then got her CPA, and worked 15-hour days during tax season, but never failed to have dinner on the table at night for her family. And she did all of this while negotiating the impossible demands and expectations of a traditional Indian man and entitled children.

I told my mom that I was dating Laura when we were sitting at her dinner table late one night in Kansas City, where she and my father had moved after leaving Cross Lanes. I was crying as I told her, uncertain as to what her response would be.

"The most important thing to me is that you are happy, Neema. I just don't want your life to be any harder than it has to be, and I worry that this will make it harder."

For a woman who was raised in a country where being gay was illegal until September of 2018, on the very day that I write this, and who spent the majority of her adulthood in the Bible Belt, this response was more than I could have asked for. But her subsequent response—her embrace of Laura, the mushy letters she sends her each birthday saying, "I'm so happy that Neema has you in her life," have proved yet again that my mom's capacity for growth, and for love, are boundless.

I was not fair to my mom growing up, unable to recognize the impossible balancing act she accomplished every day as she advanced in her education and career, and still put a traditional Gujarati dinner, with its four separately-prepared components, on the table each night. I still cringe remembering the moment as a teenager when I yelled at my mom because a piece of clothing I needed hadn't yet been ironed. As an adult, struggling to work, take care of my home, be present in my relationship, be a present and engaged aunt for my niece, I wish for my mom to bestow me with the supernatural powers she seems to possess.

Today is Dussehra—the 10th day of Navratri. After nine days of fasting, feasting, and dancing, Navratri in India ends with this tenth day off from work and school to celebrate the victory of Good over Evil. Effigies of demons get burnt in bonfires. People begin new jobs and new journeys.

This year in Boston the sky is grey and raining during Dussehra. Laura's Irish-Italian father is here for a visit, and we will spend the day together carbo-loading: starting with breakfast at a diner, followed by a beer tasting where I politely endure bitter sips of brew, and ending with three courses of pasta for dinner. It is quite possibly the least Indian of Navratri experiences that my mothers could have wished for me. Still, I know they would be proud that I am doing what they taught me to do: be family in the way that people need you to be. And though I can't stand in circle with them this Navratri, it is their faces, their voices, their presence that I feel when the first sounds of the garba come through my speakers on my drive home from work. It is them I seek to honor when I sing praises to Durga Mata.

meeting mother in the water

for goddess
Lake Michigan

RIVER COELLO

i come down to the lake
bearing gifts in the form of questions.
pachamama whispers in the tide
that she loves me, always will.
i thank her, in bittersweet tears,
for protecting me.
she draws me to her core,
gently enveloping me,
washing away my fears,
cradling me.
i ascend, levitate, swell.
we are a monster together.
we are a beauty.
the stillness brings me back
to my ancestral home in the stars,
floating safely among the debris.
i close my eyes and, behind my lids,
i reunite with the constellations
i witnessed at birth.
i am reborn in poetry and in song.
in her arms, i am endless.
sin principio, sin fin.

encontrándonos en el agua
para diosa

vengo al pie del lago
trayendo ofrendas en forma de preguntas.
pachamama susurra en la marea
que me ama, siempre me amará.
le agradezco, con lágrimas agridulces,

por protegerme.
me atrae a su núcleo,
abrazándome gentilmente,
removiendo mis miedos,
meciéndome en sus manos.
yo asciendo, levito, crezco.
juntas, somos un monstruo,
somos una belleza.
la quietud me regresa
a mi hogar ancestral en las estrellas,
flotando a salvo en las ruinas.
cierros mis ojos y, detrás de mis párpados,
me reúno con las constelaciones
que presencié en mi nacimiento.
soy renacida en poesía y canción.
en sus brazos, soy interminable.
sin principio, sin fin.

Watch me unfold

St. Louis, MO

ALYSON THOMPSON

Some may be concerned by my unfolding
My becoming may seem brutal
My journey may seem aimless or incorrect

But

My unfolding is revealing me
Remembering me
Unraveling me
Giving clarity
Until I am naked & unashamed

My becoming is a necessary brutality against all that has sought to separate
me from myself
All that has suppressed & smothered me
Promised to heal me by hurting me
Removed me from my body
Minimized my existence
Dehumanized me
Silenced me
Shamed me
Damned me

My journey has never been so guided
Never have I been so held
So loved
So aligned
So grounded
So supported
So connected

Even in the midst of the unknown
I am not lost
I know where I am going

I am going home.

Lola—A Love Story

Lincoln, Nebraska

CJ JANOVY

It's the summer of 1970 in a small Nebraska city, where our nuclear family lives in a nice ranch home. Our mom bakes us cookies and signs us up for summer reading programs, and our dad takes off his tie and plays catch with us in the yard when he gets home from work. At night in the room I share with my sister, lying in my twin bed staring at a tiny green light, I'm listening to a voice that's simple and direct: "I met her in a club down in old Soho, where you drink champagne and it tastes just like cherry-cola."

I am seven, but I understand some things. The singer is a man. He meets a woman. I know what champagne is and what happens to you when you drink it; I recognize that if it tastes like cherry cola, you'll drink a lot of it. When the singer spells out cola, "c-o-l-a, cola," I can tell he's enjoying it.

A woman walks up and asks him to dance. My late-'60s childhood has taught me that women aren't supposed to ask men to dance. But the man who's singing this story doesn't seem to mind. I find her brazenness intriguing and maybe he does too, because he asks her name. He spells it out, "L-o-l-a," and repeats it, affirms it.

Something in their interaction changes. The music gets louder and more forceful. The guitars so far have been acoustic, but now an electric one saunters in.

"Well I'm not the world's most physical guy, but when she squeezed me tight she nearly broke my spine." On Top 40 radio, getting squeezed tight is a good thing. Having your spine nearly broken doesn't sound so good, but he's singing "Oh my Lola," and in Top 40 radio music, "Oh my…" is a good thing. And he's spelling out her name again. Repeating it. Affirming it.

"Well I'm not dumb but I can't understand, why she walked like a woman and talked like a man." He's struggling with something. The feelings I'm getting from the song begin to disconnect. I'm seven, so I know the feeling of being not-dumb but not understanding something; someone walking like a woman but talking like a man doesn't confuse me because he's explaining it so matter-of-factly. Then, once again, he says she's his: "My Lola." Spells her name. Repeats it. Affirms it.

The man and the woman drink champagne and dance all night. Lola picks him up and sits him on her knee. I understand that this, too, is backwards. She must be bigger than the man who is singing, and it's a funny image. But he doesn't seem uncomfortable to be on her knee. She invites him to come home with her. This does not seem frightening because the music feels good, as if she's picking us up and carrying us with her.

"Well I'm not the world's most passionate guy, but when I looked in her eyes well I almost fell for my Lola." Now his feelings are almost confusing. If he's not that passionate, it makes sense that he "almost fell" for Lola. But then why does he call her "my Lola"? I think he fell for her. His argument with himself seems silly. Then he sings her name five times in a row, "la-la-la-la-Lola," so it's obvious how much he's fallen for her.

Then he pushes her away, he walks to the door, he falls on the floor, he gets down on his knees—any seven-year-old knows this is just the radio drama of adults in love—and then the two stare deeply into each other's eyes. This is how he always wants it to be. What he says next arrives clearly across the Midwestern airwaves.

"Girls will be boys and boys will be girls."

There's no misunderstanding these lyrics like in some other rock songs. The singer acknowledges "it's a mixed-up muddled-up shook-up world," but Lola has made it less so: "except for Lola."

He sings her name again. He knows he's young and inexperienced— having left home just a week earlier, he's never kissed a woman. But Lola smiles and takes him by the hand, tells him she's going to make him a man, and it makes him happy: He may not be "the world's most masculine man"—but who is, anyway? Not my dad. Not his friends. Not the other dads on the block or my school principal. I may not be old enough to explain his literal meaning, but I recognize the universal shrug of a regular guy, an everyman; besides, this guy's confident enough in himself: "But I know what I am and I'm glad I'm a man."

"And so is Lola."

The big reveal is less a revelation than a celebration, because he keeps singing her name. Now I know Lola is a man every time I hear the song's beginning proclamation—two long, clean, minor-but-pleasant-sounding chords followed by seven faster chords laying out the familiar tune, then surrendering to acoustic ripples as gentle as a woman's caress. And I hear the song a lot in 1970.

It is a Top 10 hit. In *Billboard*'s list of Top 100 songs for that year, "Lola" comes in at number 79. Higher than Santana's "Evil Ways," higher than Rare Earth's "(I Know) I'm Losing You," higher than Crosby, Stills, Nash & Young's "Woodstock," higher than Aretha Franklin's "Call Me."

Despite their name, the Kinks are not a queer rock band. They will eventually get more airplay with the avowed heterosexual and more masculine "You Really Got Me" and "All Day and all of the Night." But no one can argue that "Lola" doesn't fit squarely into what, during the time I spend growing up, calcifies into the macho category of Classic Rock.

It's 46 years later. I've been an out lesbian for 30 of those years. I live in Kansas City, now, working as a journalist and watching the news from all around me. It feels like a time that historians might someday describe as America's bathroom spring, when politicians seem obsessed with where transgender people can pee. In March, the North Carolina Legislature bars cities from passing ordinances protecting the rights of trans people; in May, the Obama administration sends a letter to public school districts across the country, warning them to let students use the restrooms that match their gender identity—as opposed to their genitals—or risk losing federal education funds. This infuriates leaders in more than twenty states, who sue the administration, but not before the Republican governor of South Dakota, in a surprise move, vetoes a bill similar to the one passed in North Carolina. All across the country, state legislators equipped with prefab bills provided by a national conservative organization called the Alliance Defending Freedom are pushing for transgender bathroom bans, as conservatives, enflamed by the fact that the Supreme Court legalized same-sex marriage, are casting around for any social issue on which they can claim last-stand victories in their decades-long battle against non-heterosexual people who've just wanted equal rights and protections in public life. And everyone knows that bathrooms, where Americans must go to participate in one of nature's simplest biological (dare we say God-given) processes while sublimating puritan neuroses surrounding bodily functions, are perfect places for politics: The same stoked fears that resulted in separate bathrooms for blacks and whites also worked against gays in the 1970s and have now been resurrected to stir up feelings against transgender people, a miniscule, harmless and vulnerable minority who are now in the unfortunate position of serving as proxies for liberal causes in America's endless culture wars.

Do politicians know how silly they sound, arguing that trans people in the proper bathrooms might offend women's delicate sensibilities? As if we didn't routinely have to witness, against our will, men peeing in public? But everyone knows bathrooms aren't really a problem. Even out here in the Midwest.

"I would travel through Oklahoma and go to restrooms in truck stops, and I can't think of a time when anything strange happened," remembers Allie Stoughton, who was living in Kansas when she transitioned in the late 2000s. "Even queuing up for a toilet stall in random places, people didn't glare at me." Stephanie Mott, a Christian transgender activist in Kansas who gave hundreds of talks to school, church, and civic groups before her death in 2019, had a moment in her standard presentation when she described changing clothes in a bathroom at the church where she first wore women's clothes in public. "Another transgender woman guarded the door because we didn't want a cisgender woman walking in and seeing a man in the bathroom. Turns out it wouldn't have mattered because in that church the cisgender women and the trans women mix in the bathroom. Everybody goes in there for the same reason," Mott said. "To fix our hair."

Politicians manufacturing fear and being hypocritical is nothing new, of course. Neither, at this point in America's cultural life, are transgender people, even if Caitlyn Jenner's 2015 roll-out might have made her seem like the first. That's what makes the Bathroom Spring so infuriating for those of us who have, out of necessity, spent our lives paying attention.

I was 13 when transgender tennis player Renee Richards was denied entry into the U.S. Open in 1976. I heard about that. So did Stephanie Mott. "The news of this made it all the way out to the farm where I was growing up," Mott always told audiences. Hearing about Richards when she was a kid outside of Lawrence, Kansas, was when Mott began to realize that an authentic life might be possible.

During the forty years between Richards and Jenner, Americans enjoyed enough gender ambiguity that it's ridiculous to act all shocked and offended now.

It's the fall of 1972, two years after I fell in love with "Lola." Listening to that same AM radio signal in my bedroom in Nebraska, I hear the story of a person named Holly who hitch-hikes from Florida across the U.S.A., shaving her legs along the way "and then he was a she." I am ten years old when Lou Reed's "Walk on the Wild Side" peaks at No. 16 on *Billboard's*

charts. If "Lola" gave me my first understanding that girls could be boys and boys could be girls, "Walk on the Wild Side" answers my childhood questions about how it was done. For the rest of the '70s and '80s, I watch and listen as society embraces the "gender benders" David Bowie, Boy George and Annie Lenox, who all have huge hits. (Much later, I will come to understand that Little Richard, now far past his peak in the 1950s, was a class unto himself.).

I watch as movies jump on the bandwagon. In 1992, *The Crying Game* gets six Oscar nominations, including best supporting actor for Jaye Davidson, who played the transgender love interest, and best actor for Stephen Rea, who falls in love with the transgender character; it wins for best original screenplay. In 1993, *Mrs. Doubtfire* wins a Golden Globe for Best Picture (Musical/Comedy) and its man-dressing-as-a-woman star, Robin Williams, wins Best Actor (Musical/Comedy).

By now I've met transgender people in Kansas City, where I've settled down and built a career. Even though the trans women who show up to political meetings are among those who do the most work, we still call our struggle "the lesbian- and gay-rights movement." It will be a while before we add letters to convey the wide spectrum of sexual orientation and gender identity. It'll be even longer until Hollywood begins to atone for what is actually a long history of dramatic sins against trans people.

It's the fall of 2016. I am in my 50s. Watching TV one night, I see a cisgender, heterosexual actor named Jeffrey Tambor accept an Emmy for playing a transgender woman named Maura on Amazon's series "Transparent." In the show, it's the real transgender people surrounding Maura who are the most likeable, in striking contrast to the self-absorbed, energy-sucking cis members of Maura's family.

It's been a couple of years since *Time* magazine decided that America had reached a "Transgender Tipping Point," declaring equality and respect for trans people to be "America's Next Civil Rights Frontier." On *Time*'s cover was Laverne Cox, who plays one of the most compelling characters on Netflix's "Orange is the New Black." With Cox, trans people's new visibility is a thing of literal beauty. The camera flashes to Cox as Tambor gives his speech.In this moment, Tambor has extraordinary power: He demands, and receives, a stop to the music that begins to play as he runs out of time for his speech. He demands that producers and network owners and agents "give transgender talent a chance. Give them auditions. Give them their stories. Do that." And another thing: . "I would not be unhappy were I the last cisgender male to play a female transgender on television." Applause rises boisterously, and the music does not begin again until Tambor starts to walk away from the podium. Watching from the couch a thousand miles away, this nationally televised starburst of support for trans stories and trans people is an astounding thing to witness.

It's also not as simple as it appears. In the year ahead, cast members will raise allegations of Tambor's sexual harassment. Creator Jill Soloway will end the show with a two-hour musical in which Maura is dead. *The Wall Street Journal* will later report that the series had fewer than a million viewers—a disappointment in big-media world, but among those million viewers are countless trans people who've had their existence validated in the fully human characters surrounding the insufferable Pfeffermans.

Still, there is an ongoing litany of trans people, almost all of them trans women of color, murdered across the country. At least 27 are dead by November's election, which inflicts upon us a new president who will methodically obliterate hard-won progress on every imaginable front.

It's June 2019. Nearly fifty years have passed since I first heard "Lola." A woman named Danica Roem serves as the first openly transgender person elected to a state legislature. To win the seat, she defeated a Virginia Republican who'd held it for a quarter of a century, and who had called himself the state's "chief homophobe" and introduced a bathroom bill, in a race that wasn't even close. But up in Vermont, the first openly trans woman to run for governor of any state, Democrat Christine Hallquist, lost badly to Republican Phil Scott—but Scott isn't typical of Republicans these days. "Scott supports abortion rights, transgender rights and LGBTQ protections," the Burlington Free Press notes, chalking up his wide margin of victory to the fact that Vermonters like the familiarity of incumbents. Scott signs legislation requiring that all single-user public bathrooms in the state be marked as gender-neutral. "For many transgender and gender non-conforming Vermonters, having single stalled bathrooms labeled 'male' or 'female' creates social stress and discomfort, or instances where you face hostility and mistreatment including verbal and emotional abuse," he says at the signing ceremony. "Treating others this way is not who we are as Vermonters and I hope that signing this bill will send a powerful message that that's not the way we act."

The actors in "Pose," meanwhile, have helped us quickly move beyond "Transparent." This year brings six Emmy nominations for the powerful series about New York City's 1980s ballroom culture. Trans icon Janet Mock is one of the producers, and the series boasts the largest cast of trans people so far.

"Trans women and men of America, of the world, we got this. I love y'all," one of the stars, Dominique Jackson, says on Instagram after the nominations are announced. (On awards night, only one cast member takes home a statue: Billy Porter makes history as the first openly gay black man to win lead actor in a drama.)

By 2020, we have a status report on all of this entertainment. Cox is among the executive producers of a Netflix documentary called *Disclosure*, which recounts a century of Hollywood depicting trans people as jokes, deceivers and monsters. Measuring progress through the entertainment industry turns out to be as fraught as measuring it through politics.

Now trans people are beginning to tell their own stories, which are so much better than the ones we already enjoyed. Still, Cox says, "I wonder if people who watch and love these shows, I wonder if they will reach out to trans people in need and work to defeat policies that scapegoat us, policies that discriminate against us, policies that dehumanize us. Because until that happens, all that energy from the silver screen won't be enough to better the lives of trans people off the screen."

It shouldn't have been this hard. Fifty years ago, when no one would let trans people speak for themselves, the presumably straight, cisgender men in the Kinks stated the obvious so plainly even a seven-year-old kid in Nebraska could hear it.

Boys will be girls and girls will be boys. It's a mixed up world. We know this in our hearts, where we always feel the beat. Politicians try to trick us, but love songs don't lie.

Your Father's Car

Skokie, IL

GREGG SHAPIRO

You are driving your father's car. An orange 1975 AMC Hornet station wagon. The one with the black vinyl interior that gets so hot in the summer that your skin hurts just thinking about sitting in it or touching the steering wheel. And in the winter, the vinyl becomes so brittle that you are afraid to apply your full weight to the seats for fear of cracking them like ice chips. You are driving your father's car because your mother wears the key to her car—a lemon-yellow 1976 Lincoln Continental with a white vinyl top—around her neck on a gold chain, as if it was a religious medallion.

At first, it doesn't matter to you where you drive, as long as it is away from your parents' house and the nightly dinner-time disagreements. Away from the eat-in kitchen with the lime green wallpaper, the sink with the coughing drain pipes, and the supermarket-purchased dinnerware. Where the latest in a series of ongoing mealtime melees leaves you with the desire to join the Hare Krishnas, the Jews for Jesus, or any other group that would have you.

Tonight's fracas is about the volume at which you play your stereo in your bedroom. Does it really matter that it is Barry Manilow's *Even Now* album? That most of your friends are blasting Led Zeppelin and Judas Priest and Black Sabbath from their speakers, while the fact that your record collection leans toward Manilow and Bette Midler, the 5th Dimension and The Carpenters, is never even mentioned.

After storming away from the dinner table with all the delinquent drama you can muster, you throw yourself onto the lower bunk in the bedroom you share with your older brother and press your face into your pillow, wondering as you have before, how long you would have to stay in that position before you suffocate. But you don't want to give them the satisfaction of dying under their roof. You want to make them suffer. You want to go missing, end up hustling on the streets like Leigh McCloskey in *Alexander: The Other Side of Dawn.*

Initially, you stay close to home, driving a block over to Lee-Wright Park to see who is hanging out by the basketball courts. It's the usual collection of stoner jocks, perched on the back of the painted park bench, their

Converse All-Starred feet firmly planted on the seat. Johnny and Scott and Bobby and Matthew in cut-offs of varying lengths and t-shirts exposing biceps and clinging to pectorals of different sizes. Johnny and Bobby are on the wrestling team, muscular and swift, and unbeknownst to the other, each has taken his turn wrestling with you. Not on the mat at the school gym, but on the carpeted floors of their bedrooms and later in their beds.

These are just a couple of the secrets you keep as you drive your father's car through the alley and pull up behind the park bench and come to a stop. Scott looks over his shoulder at you and nods in acknowledgment. He runs track and field and as he leans forward from his position on the park bench, his t-shirt rides up a little over his slim hips and you can see that he is still wearing his white bike jockstrap under his shorts. You are familiar with the way it fits him, having helped him in and out of it on numerous occasions. Scott is fast, but you are faster.

Matthew's still mad at you about the hickey incident. He won't meet your eyes in the hall at school and he won't meet them now. He doesn't understand passion or desire, abandon and free falling, the heat of the moment. He understands the pummel horse, the rings, the parallel bars, the trampoline. You understand the tramp part.

The four of them together like this floods your mouth with a salty taste. You look in the side-view mirror to make sure you are not drooling. After a few minutes, you pull away without saying anything and are surprised to see them each waving goodbye to you in the rearview mirror.

You push the last button on the radio and watch the red line slide to the end of the dial and come to a stop at WGCI. You turn on the radio, hoping to hear "Boogie Oogie Oogie" by A Taste of Honey, but settle for "Macho Man" by the Village People. This music makes you think of the city and so you drive your father's car towards New Town, the intersection of Belmont and Broadway.

The fake ID Johnny made for you has gotten you into a few of the bars downtown, like Alfie's and the Bistro, and also a couple in New Town, including the Broadway Limited and Center Stage. You've never told him where you go and he's never asked. This arrangement works well for everyone concerned.

You are letting your father's car decide where you will go. It's a game you play, where you pretend the steering wheel is a planchette and the street is a Ouija board. You operate the gas pedal and the brakes, but you have no idea what your final destination will be. Tonight, as it turns out, it's the Glory Hole on Wells Street in Old Town. After a couple of swings around the block, you pull into a parking space a few doors from the entrance.

No sooner are you in the door, where the doorman glances at your fake ID with all the disinterest he can muster, than you feel several sets of eyes on you. You find a wall to lean against and reach into your back pocket for your cigarettes. You have only recently mastered smoking without coughing or getting sick. It feels like an accomplishment, like learning a foreign language or losing a few pounds on a diet.

You don't need to diet or put on a few pounds. You are, as most of the daddies in the Glory Hole would attest, just right. When you aren't slouching, you are easily six feet tall. You have a swimmer's build, even though you hate swimming. You have dirty blonde hair, that you wear parted in the middle, slightly feathered. You have an unobtrusive nose, a strong chin and jaw-line, full lips, straight white teeth, and an attractive smile.

Your eyes are blue, but you've seen them cloud over and turn grey in the mirror when things don't go your way or you are deep in thought. Like tonight, when you stood before your reflection in the bathroom mirror, plotting your temporary exit from suburbia, knowing full well that it was futile to ask for permission to borrow your father's car.

After running through a few scenarios, one of which included dipping your hand into your father's pants pocket, while he took his post-feast nap on the couch in the den, you slip quietly out of the bathroom, out the back door of the house, and into the garage. Your father, who has locked his key in the car on more than one instance, keeps a spare in a magnetic case under the hood. You retrieve it, smooth as Robert Wagner in *It Takes a Thief*, and make your stealthy retreat.

You light the cigarette and let it dangle from your lips, the smoke causing you to squint. You thrust your hands in the pockets of your new Calvin Klein jeans and try to strike a provocative pose. You are waiting for someone to come over and offer to buy you a drink. You don't wait long.

Knowing that you still have to drive your father's car to your next destination, whether it is home or to wherever the night takes you, you ask for a Perrier, with a twist of lime. You are intent on keeping your wits about you. You make small talk with the man who buys you the bottle of fizzy water. It is hard to make out many details about him in the dimly lit bar. He could be anywhere between your age and death. He rests a hand, big and powerful, on your chest. You feel the warmth through the fabric of your t-shirt, which bears the name of your high school. You are teetering between arousal and boredom. You think he may be slurring his words, at least the ones you can hear over the loud music. He leans in to kiss you in what seems like slow motion. You turn your head and he licks your earlobe. You thank him for the drink and find another section of wall against which to position yourself for optimal viewing and display.

A man just a little taller than you slides over slightly to make room for you. You raise your green Perrier bottle as a sign of thanks. He raises his green bottle of Rolling Rock in a return salute. The next thing you know he is standing directly in front of you, looking into your eyes. You don't mind as he is much better looking, and maybe even less drunk, than the other guy. You move your mouth towards his but stop short of contact. He mimics you. You try to suppress a smile. He does the same. Your crotches meet. There is electricity. They stay pressed together like magnets and ball bearings. You imagine what your legs would look like resting on his shoulders.

When he tells you that he lives around the corner, the first and only thing he has said to you in the ten minutes that you have stood like this, groin to groin, you are grateful not to have to get in your father's car and drive anywhere. You wonder how you would have explained the orange Hornet to this man, to any man. You aren't even sure that you can still explain it to yourself. You dream of the day when the orange Hornet will lose its sting.

"Your Father's Car" was first published in 2013 in Issue 04 of *Jonathan: Gay Men's Fiction* and was included in my short story collection *Lincoln Avenue* (Squares & Rebels, 2014).

The Island

Allentown, PA

EDWARD M. COHEN

In the middle of my home town—Allentown, PA—there is a park where the married men come to cruise and the middle aged queens come to watch. I suppose there is a park like it in every small town in America; islands bypassed by Gay Liberation.

The marrieds do not get out of their cars. I suppose they are afraid to be seen. They have left their sleeping wives at home with a story about walking the dog or buying a paper, and circle the park in their minivans, sometimes stopping with the motor idling. Sometimes turning down a side street, looking for someone to blow, or be blown by. Sometimes to pay, sometimes for free. One guy is a foot fetishist and he is looking for someone to walk on his chest. The local Elvis impersonator is a voyeur and his car follows the others around. In a place like Allentown, everyone knows everyone else.

There is a cadre of boys who come to get picked up; some on bike, some on foot. Some are newly arrived in town; some have been here for years. The high school dropouts who clerk at Macdonald's lounge under the trees after work.

"You do it for the money?" I asked one kid.

Ordinarily, the hustlers talk to the hustlers and we queens talk to one another but, this night, I'd come out early so there were only the two of us, with no cars circling, and he seemed as lonely as I.

"I've got a job," he snarled.

"Where?"

"Lehigh Valley Hospital."

"Doing what?"

"Washing dishes."

"You like it?"

"It's okay."

"How long you been at it?"

"Seven years."

The pay was lousy, he added, which was why he had started to come to the park. Also, there was not much to do in Allentown at night if you were poor and had no TV. He had a girlfriend but she was pregnant which was why he was coming out so early because things were going from bad to worse and he was getting scared. I told him I knew the feeling.

We have our junkies in Allentown and the cops drive by but they don't do much until one of the homeowners complains about the circling cars. Around two in the morning it can get pretty noisy. Then, the cops flash their lights in our eyes as they pass but we preen and murmur, "Another close-up, Mr. DeMille?" and there is nothing more they can do.

We know our rights as an oppressed minority. The oppressed of the oppressed because even the gay kids, on their way to the clubs, hoot at us from their cars. We embarrass the marrieds and the hustlers don't like us because we never have any money.

Which explains why, the next night when I saw the dishwasher, he and I didn't say hello. But that was okay because my buddies showed up to sit on the benches and gossip and giggle and sing themes from "I Love Margie" and "Bonanza." Only fifteen minutes away, there is this hip club, where the kids are heading, where everyone dances with everyone else; gays with gays, gays with girls, straight guys with gay guys, and the gays even kiss on the dance floor.

But we old timers came out when things were different and habits die hard. We don't even like to dance with one another and, as far as two middle aged queens having sex; once, I went to bed with a guy from the bench and it turned out he had shaved all his pubic hair. He had heard that it grew back thicker and he wanted his crotch to look like Robert Mitchum's.

"I hate to tell you this," I sighed, "but I think Robert Mitchum is dead."

Those were the good old days, he replied, when you cruised in secret and had to watch for the cops. Once, he told me, he eyed this stud on the street and they both looked over their shoulders as they passed, good sign number one. Then, they stopped and did the cloak and dagger number, staring into a shop window, peering sideways, never smiling. Finally, they started the "You live around here? - You live alone?" tap dance. Street cruising is a forgotten art, we agreed, and none of the kids today could have survived way back then for a second!

This stud finally asked "You wanna fuck?" and my pal answered, "Sure," and bingo, out came the badge and the cuffs since the stud was from Vice.

Only, the queen didn't panic because he knew the laws about entrapment. They wouldn't let him make bail until morning, but he stayed up all night in his jail cell and, next morning, he told the judge that the cop had said, "You wanna fuck?" and if that wasn't entrapment, what was?

"Besides, Your Honor, I'm a red blooded American boy. My friend asked if I wanted to fuck, I thought he meant girls!"

Smart faggot. Stupid cop. Case dismissed. Things like that made you proud in the old days because life was so tough. You could get robbed. You could get blackmailed. You could get V.D. and pass it on to your wife.

I blew him anyway, though he looked like a plucked chicken to me. That was the way we were brought up. You fulfilled your responsibilities and finished what you started. Some things change but not what's right and wrong.

We queens don't like the noise in the dance club. We can't talk over the music. We miss the slow dances. The crowd is too young. The kids are too cliquey. The bar is too expensive. The drinks are watered. Here, we buy a six-pack and the evening is set. Most of our parents are dead so it is no big deal who knows and who doesn't but we don't believe in telling the world. If we kissed on the dance floor, someone would see. Someone would talk and who needs the gossip? We do not discuss our home lives at work, except for what we ate last night and what shows we watched on TV. Two school teachers who have been lovers for thirty years have told the town that they live together because they are brothers-in-law and nobody asks any questions. The kids say we should come out of the shadows but we like to be where we always have been. That's why I like the park. I like to talk in disconnected circles to guys who know what I mean. I like to think about the past in shared silence. Old friends. The gossip. The songs. I like the cool breeze. The steady hum of the cars. The play of the headlights in the dark.

And, years from now, at the supermarket, when I spot the snarling dishwasher, carrying the baby his girlfriend is carrying now, not to worry, buddy, I know the rules. Nobody says hello.

An earlier version on The Island, under another title, appeared in *Down In The Dirt*.

Steam

Columbus, OH and Grant County, IN

JOEL SHOWALTER

Tonight the heat persists, and yet I sit in the
steam room at the downtown Y, counting
and recounting the graying tiles on the dim
walls, on the floor, evading

and catching the glances of the near-naked
men, all of us silent, listening for the hiss of the
apparatus, the dispensation of the
blistering mist. My gaze falls

on the thin skin at my wrist, the hairs there darkened
in the thick, sodden air, delicate whorls, almost
black, twisted, damp, and my sight shifts suddenly
to pictures from last night:

shucking the ears of sweet corn at the sink, the
dark, wild tangle at the husk's peak and the fine
fibers between the rows of pearls, wet threads
that cluster on the counter,

the simmering water sending its own steam
into the kitchen and, further, into my memory:
my mother in another August, boiling water
for corn, picked fresh

from the garden stalk and quickly stripped, this
supper by lamplight and the TV's spark, my
father's face, hard as baked earth, slow fans
murmuring at the windows, the room taut

and still as a thief, expectant, poised, like the
dried kernels, stained pink with poison, that

we dropped into soil, row after row, in the
spring, my father and I, our backs
and necks slick with sweat, weary, unspeaking—
like these men around me now, who tense their
muscles in this shadowed room, testing the
invisible filaments that stretch between

us in the heat, that promise or threaten to
connect or ensnare us, like spider silk,
 glinting in the intermittent light, waiting
for rain that offers no relief.

"Steam" was first published by *Mud Season Review.*

Excerpts from the memoirs of Gene Dawson

GENE DAWSON

Parnell, Iowa, 1951

About this same time, I had seen an ad in some paper for *Little Blue Books—Information on Everything* by E. Haldeman-Julius with a Kansas address. Needless to say, I ordered them and was astounded and amazed at their contents! They were so full of taboo information that I hid them in a compartment of the threshing machine that was in winter storage in the corn crib. I would sneak a few in to read at night in my locked bedroom—it was the only room and closet in the house that could be locked. The perfect room for me! I shared most of this "knowledge" with Leroy, who was 17 and a senior at Parnell High School. Somehow I knew that Kenny and my Parnell and Holbrook gang members should not share my secrets.

From this information, I found a listing of "Controversial" books for sale and ordered *The Homosexual in America* and some *Sexology* magazines. I felt bewildered, guilt and shame upon reading the book and coming to the conclusion that I was never going to change and be like Kenny and my buddies and have girlfriends, a wife and children. I would have to lead a double life and always be on guard or be ostracized by family, friends, community and church. I determined I would erase from my mind all "perverse" thoughts and force myself to be "normal" … not realizing that so-called "normal" was not normal for me.

Many years later, I realized that at least 40 percent of my buddies were probably bisexual and some of the men in the small Irish community were actually gay. That was a word I never heard in rural Iowa. People were labled "odd" or "queer" (a word I detest). I announced to Leroy that "I know I am one of those and I think you are, too." So from then on and even actually before, Leroy and I always had a common secret bond. At least we had each other for support and confidential discussions.

On the Road, 1953

On Sept. 11, Don Shomler, who I had stayed in contact with since our first meeting at the Hurdle & Halter Inn in 1951, invited me to go on vacation with him to Miami. It would cost me nothing—he just wanted my company. I said good-bye to dear Mother, Dad and my wonderful Brothers—little Marion Thomas had just started school. I was overjoyed to be through with farm labor and thought, "I'll never have to make hay or fence or lift another bale again!" Little did I know.

I wasn't even reluctant to leave my pigeons behind—they lived in the barn loft and cattle shed and could take care of themselves. I packed three suitcases that held all the possessions I owned and Kenny drove me to Cedar Rapids.

Don and I spent our first night in Dubuque, Iowa, and then it was on to Chicago and the gay clubs on Clark and Division streets. In Cleveland, I saw my first drag (female impersonator) show and was thrilled to meet the performers who, to me, were like movie stars! Our stop in Buffalo, N.Y. was uneventful and I was not impressed with Niagara Falls. It reminded me of flushing a huge toilet with the water cascading and tumbling down the falls. To heck with the scenery, I wanted to get to where there was action!

St. Louis, Missouri, 1954

I had been introduced to the "Stork Clubz' on the outskirts of East St. Louis where I knew the performers who were all female impersonators with names like Georgia White, Gaye Dawn, Stormy Day and Sunny Day. After the shows, the "girls" and their boyfriends, who were ex-cons and extremely handsome in my estimation, would go to the "Blue Flame" and the "Ritz," two clubs that were in the ghetto. In fact, Gaye Dawn (Ralph Calves) was very jealous of me and I was not allowed to sit anywhere near her guy, Sonny. She didn't need to worry because I was never one to be known as a homewrecker—I didn't want it done to me and it had been. Some insecure individuals delight to "Steal your man" or break people up. Not me!

But at the two clubs in East St. Louis, the Black bars' owners and patrons treated us like celebrities. They had great music and very talented acts from the "Harlem Club" in Brooklyn, Ill. There was open gambling, dice, betting and games in the back rooms. Some of the African American gentlemen would occasionally ask me to touch or pitch the dice for them. I had no idea what was a "good" number.

It got to the point that I would hitch a ride or walk the Mississippi River bridge to get to East St. Louis to drink and play at the black clubs. Some of the white guys began calling me the "African Queen," a movie showing at the time. Of course, it was said haughtily and derisively as most of them were highly prejudiced. Even Ms. Jennie, Ms. Pierre and Chuck Burton, another friend, thought I was going a little too far when I ventured there alone.

There were two Caucasian detectives on the East St. Louis police force who hated gays and Blacks. If they would spy us in a Black bistro, they would arrest us and take us for a terrific amount of harassment and outright obscene suggestions of what arts we were supposedly performing with "█████"—their word. We were berated and called the lowest of the low—even beneath whale shit, which is at the bottom of the ocean. We would eventually be released and told not to come back to East St. Louis again.

Of course, we went back and the Saturday night before Easter 1954, Ms. Jennie, Chuck, "Ms." David Grayson, Ms. Pierre and I were arrested and lodged in the black womens' section of the East St. Louis jail. On Easter morning, a Salvation Army woman tried to preach to us on our "lowliness," but was shouted down. That evening, with no money, we were released to find our way across the Mississippi River. The detectives had confiscated all of our "gay shekels."

Skinny little blondes

Chicago, IL

ELIZABETH HARPER

Skinny little blondes,
skin like parchment paper,
want me to do things to them
in bathroom stalls across the nation.

I'll leave them with bruises,
with things to think about,
things to do. I'll leave them
always wanting more.

So easy to play at love,
so easy to kiss, to hurt,
to leave them wanting more.

Thirst

Cleveland, OH

CHRISTOPHER GONZALEZ

You're on the freeway with your mom for the first time in a year and there are hardly any flurries in the sky. She's playing catch up about the family and church, about the house in disarray. *It's a mess,* she warns. *I don't want to hear your mouth.* She's all smiles when she says it, though. Then asks *how is everything? Things are cool,* you say. You return to your phone; thumb through Twitter. Your body is angled away from her and you're not aware of it until you look up from the screen, and realize you're practically facing her from the passenger seat. José Altuve is the current background on your phone. It's a weak attempt at passing: if anyone asks, you're supposed to say you're an Astros fan, but in such close proximity to your mom you fear the lie won't hold and you assume this protective position.

You exit Twitter and Altuve stares back, taunting you. He's got a base-ball glove on and he's making a fist with his free hand. The picture was taken a second before his skin touched the leather. His beard is crisp and his forearm firm, strong. There's a ripple of vein, and you daydream about the various ways he could choke you out, or run his hand through your hair. You crave access to that hand off the diamond, away from your phone. The car meets a red light and you're thinking about how you would lick the salty sweat from his fingers if he let you.

When you're home for the holidays, you watch Hallmark movies with your mom. Stories mostly about small town white men falling for big city white women that result in both parties trapping one another in an environment without Seamless, public transportation, good coffee, or their realized selves. And the thing you find most upsetting is the lack of real kissing and sex, even implied sex, for characters this straight, this cloyingly attractive: Lacey Chabert, Christina Milian, Victor Webster, Antonio Cupo, Alicia Witt, Tatyana Ali, Jonathan Bennett, Alexa and Carlos PenaVega, for Christ's sake. All rendered into sexless, sweatered mannequins.

The male lead in tonight's movie is Mario Lopez. He plays opposite Melissa Joan Hart who you've crushed on since *Sabrina*, although her recent roles have been questionable. She has a monologue twenty minutes in and you watch her through a side eye. *Mario Lopez's dimples deserve top billing*, you'd like to say, but don't. Instead you bundle it into a tweet for your cyber friends.

In between rolling socks and scrolling through Facebook, your mom drinks Christmas coquito from a snowman mug. You sip craft beer, try to guess which plot points the movie will hit next. Often, there's a throwaway character, a shopkeeper, who speaks with a slight lisp and dresses fashionably well for a small town—you want to follow that guy's thread, but that isn't Hallmark's formula.

Mario Lopez enters a diner; the camera zooms in on his buttery soft face. That's the formula. He's wearing a green Henley and you make a note to find a screenshot later. Your mom looks up at Mario Lopez, adjusts her glasses. She laughs. *He's so cute*, she says above a whisper, then laughs again, this time more loudly. A sock hits you on the neck and she feigns innocence. These are the moments you wonder if she knows. You envy her comfort with expressing thirst, how being so openly parched became a mom thing. Now, the camera is on Melissa Joan Hart. Her scowl flashes across the screen; she's confused and a little pissed off at Mario Lopez. The scene changes and your opportunity fades with it.

It wasn't always José Altuve on your phone. Before, there was Oscar Isaac. It wasn't his arms or hands that reeled you in, but his lips and eyes, and his curls in full bloom, that glorious mane occupying prime real estate beneath your phone's digital clock. There was three months with Chris Pine and half a year with Lin-Manuel Miranda. There was Prince Harry, Donald Glover, Richard Madden with the Fiji water girl, Gael García Bernal, Pedro Pascal, Bruno Mars, Steven Yeun in an $1100 bat sweater. There was Colin Firth reclining in a bathtub; Jack Black in sweatpants, sipping white wine; a salt-and-peppered Alfonso Cuarón holding his three Academy awards, bow tie undone. Slim men, thick men, chiseled beards, blue eyes, dark eyes, all welcomed, given equal opportunity on your phone's lock and home screens. An oasis retrievable from the pocket of your jeans.

That night, long after your mom goes to sleep, when the house settles, you masturbate furiously in a bed that doesn't belong to you. A tiny twin-size in the guest room. Holding the laptop with your left hand, you stroke yourself with the right. All you can think about before coming is how exhausting everything is. You watch porn in a private browser and hide your dating apps in a folder on the third window of your phone. You send nudes and pray they don't reach unkind hands, that the receivers might treasure your photos the way you treasure your own digital menagerie of men. And really, it's not the fact that you basically always but sometimes don't fantasize about the men on your phone. It's your own spirit you wish to access. And preserve. You're able to contain the pure joy that bubbles in your heart when you glance at the screen. You get to let your imagination linger in the ether.

Finished, you wipe your hand clean on a blanket and sit up with the laptop. Its brightness is on the lowest possible setting before the screen turns black. You like this dim, blue glow. You enjoy the experience of looking into it without a reflection, without the worry of seeing a defined shape of yourself staring back.

"Thirst" originally appeared in the online literary journal *Hobart.*

To Love the Horseman of Famine

Cleveland, OH

DOMINICK DUDA

He wore nothing extraordinary—jeans
& a cardigan, traveled from his modest grotto
to my doorstep & so the story unfolds:

Touch begat touch, adamantine desire,
our bodies took root against the hallway wall.
I decided to make him mine. All winter

we fed each other pomegranate seeds, one by one,
pressed dirt into our navels, woke breathless
& sweating every night. By spring I lost ten pounds,

his torso filled. A husband fermenting just for me.
What he lacked in honesty could be forgiven
by his smile. I begged him for a harvest,

for his hands, & he took me to a field, slaughtered
his horse, made me drag the twitching corpse home.

The Ironwood Experiment

Ironwood, MI

RAYMOND LUCZAK

Once upon a time I believed my hometown's
landmarks would never evaporate like fog
rushing in to erase everything as if
    never existed,
but they have. St. Michael's Church is now a
parking lot facing the new police station.
The gas station at McLeod and Suffolk has
    been paved over with
asphalt: another parking lot. The building
behind it has vanished into more asphalt.
Pawnshops and thrift stores have proliferated,
    remnants of a town
that doesn't like to recall what it's like now,
preferring a time when mining companies
pulled tonnages of iron ore as if from
    air instead of earth
and loaded them onto trains for ports elsewhere,
making a name for themselves in many war
efforts. Then the earth had nothing left to give.
    The town is a master
illusionist, making big buildings vanish
as if in the blink of an eye. Norrie School,
which took up half a large block, has turned into
    a green carpet of
vacancy, surrounded by houses that still
echo ghost-children who played in recess.
This, here, is the Ironwood Experiment:
    let's see how many
childhood landmarks can be rounded up and tossed
into the Super-Sargasso Sea, a place
where all the lost things go, and where memories
    can be priced for cash.
But the universe isn't any pawnshop.

We're in hock to the mysterious forces
that may or may not honor consignment deals.
    Once it's gone, it's gone,
lingering in our brains' synapses firing
its last breaths of memory trying to save
ourselves from the eventuality of
    this land under sea.

as above so below

Peoria, IL

LARS AVIS

i've been feeling pretty bored out here,
like out here doesn't grip the sediment of

the illinois river bed and its vacant warehouses
don't cast their shadows over s. w. washington street

and into the murky water. like out here feels akin
to an estranged family member of a ghost town

wrapped in the company of cornfields, no
longer on speaking-terms. out here is as

present as its inhabitants; that is, absent without
a doctor's note inside an at-will state. i reside out

here inside a once-whiskey city, drunk on fumes
and years-removed from all those whose poster ghosts

haunt my walls, bracing for an autumn
afternoon run amongst rows of headstones

and sepultures of springdale, tripping over
sassafras tree roots on the way to the bottom

of the cemetery, allowing mud to clot the
grooves of my boot soles because i didn't

pause to scrape it off onto the curb. some would argue
it's not a flyover state i am engulfed in, but rather a thing

built up and worn down over thousands of years borne
by deposits seeping lazily to strain themselves through

coffee-ground soil to calcify a resting place of chasms
and eroding darkness below the surface. what do i seek

from the Divine? when my *out here* tips these balances
to embody *in there,* will my mundanity prove to be enough?

Before there was, blink

Cedar Falls, Iowa

JOCELYN KRUEGER

The rain slowly began to erase him. There was no light, the wet its covering. Small rivulets of water merged with his skin and ran down his body, pushing him from view. Pushing him away to a distance past what is real. James looked deeper somehow, further away and dripping downward into where he stood. This spot of summertime forts, of escape, of our dance, our land but now too a place that dripped away.

My legs plunged with it. There was a collapse inward and I felt my newly declared girlhood drifting, inward and outward.

Inward and outward.

There was water between us.

I stopped seeing. I knew he was there, the night wasn't old, I knew him. I knew his flesh, we had just touched, he was just here, but my vision became empty.

"James?" my voice reached out, quiet and unsure if it could be heard. Rain dripped from my lips. Beads of it stretched across my mouth as I said his name. It was cold and sticky. I wondered if I was erasing too but quickly realized the distant street lights behind him made me, my skin, more visible at that moment. Luminous gleams pressed strongly against me. I had shown myself but now I felt unwillingly illuminated and exposed. I wanted to look past my own drenched body and see James, but the blinding light reflected off my form back into my eyes. I had not erased. I was revealed and was being seen more than I'd ever been before.

The lamplight was gentler with James. It was his light, not mine. It had checked in on him and his sister while they slept, watched him get on the school bus on early winter mornings, and tucked its incandescent blanket securely around his apartment complex. In the darkening rain, the light cast out, reaching across the grass and against his back, deepening the shadows of his face. The light was pulling him back.

In that twilight call from home, water rendered my pink shirt clear and I felt naked before him. I felt a still emptying wetness. Water was replacing friendship. Droplets and streams pooled and ran across my body. I was immobile, unable to reach out to James. I didn't know if he was still there and I did not want, in that moment, to be all alone with my body. I hoped for a sign of life, waiting drenched and seeking any sign of James' presence.

I began to feel his breath, and it felt like drying off. A momentary presence from the void as his own inward and outward air touched me or left me.

"James?" I asked again, this time a bit louder, a bit drier. This time to ask who he was, who we were. The breath from the void moved up my face. It was gentler. It brushed my eyes. I blinked.

There was a thin white crack where his face had melted. Teeth, his teeth, James' teeth. My friend I hoped was there, must be.

He must have been moving slowly backward, he must have been supporting me, holding my hands. At that moment, my arms dropped. We were trees in the thicket and I fell away, crashing while he stood still. The weight of my arms joined the rest of me, falling absently to my side. I became cold.

"James?" louder still. I planted myself and could feel the ground again. I looked out and could see again too. James' dark silhouette was misted between the trees. Far behind him, the streetlight would catch his bare torso and shoot damp beams into my eyes. I blinked a lifetime of blinks.

I would later learn that blinking is tied to how we remember, like bookmarking your thoughts and experiences for future recall. Now I wish I had blinked less as a young girl. The violence throughout my life towards my girlhood hangs pearlescent over my memories.

Or maybe I could have blinked more, more than a lifetime of eye shuttering. Maybe that could have given me power over my memories. Cut them into such tiny pieces that any single part could be removed and leave no trace visible in the wholeness of self.

That's not how it works. There is no magic to it, no special powers or controls. It must be solace enough to hold on to the knowledge that memory isn't real. Only forgetting is real.

Some moments I wish to forget. That moment of the inward and outward vacuity, the wet and distant lumens, me and James, a moment when I was never more sure of my femininity and aloneness, was not one of them. The moment to forget had not yet blinked.

"James!" I pleaded with him to know me, to acknowledge my presence. The repetition of his name was wearing, distance stretched and he slowly backed towards his home, away from a girl laid bare, new, open, and wet. Why must I call and name him so he can name me?

"James," I said. "Just…"

"I..."

"Just, just say something."

"I... I can't..." He turned and ran away.

I was left with his declaration of self while the revelation of mine was left hanging. The weight of it stalled me, left my body present in the thicket and the rain. A solitary girl unable to move.

I stood in the place where we had just swirled. It is somewhere that escape and dynamic truths revealed should have led to deeper understandings. Instead my first and only friendship had been rendered fragile. This is where dancing and movement used to go around and around and up and out. Now it was all down and away. Even the sky and light participated in this new and terrible motion Down and away.

This was where I'd taken a party of dolls and toys and then shared warm teas, a dulcet bond between girls imagined. Some were still here, now sharing in my dampness.

This was where I'd dropped the cinderblock on my toe, and hidden my bloodied and limping body—like so many other things—from my parents. In the rain shower, the pain was much deeper than any I'd known could exist. The cinderblock was still there too. It reached out to me and I sat.

I looked down at my toes as they wiggled in the mud. You could not see where they had been struck by the block; they were unblemished. My limp too, having vanished in the months previous, I realized then had been absent from my thoughts as I came to know James and myself that summer. When you're hurting, sometimes it's a sharing that heals, or maybe you can't be aware of your healing. I did not know. There was a lot that was gone, and girl, had I shared it.

Even at that moment, every time I squelched down my feet, the rain and the light refused to mudden me, to show me anything but healing.

I did not want to lose him. I looked up and James was a distant dot, a torso swimming in the grass, arms flailing wildly as he neared the street lights of his apartment complex. He ran different now, almost towards something rather than away.

I could catch him. I knew I was faster and I could catch him.

Before I realized I had stood up, I was running. I knew how to move here. The prairie and my body had an understanding, one grown out of seasons of practice. I knew wintered snow drifts and lumpy clumps of grasses that left warm cavities. These would collapse with your tread, causing you to stumble but they also offered respite and shelter from the open and biting wind should you crawl inside. This landscape, now, I could run through. Spring growth and autumnal debris persisted across years. The materials for James' and my fort shelter for wildlife witnesses. This I ran through with an ethereal fleetness that could only mean my body had temporarily lost all substance.

As I gained on James, I did not feel the grasses' saw-edges. And on a cloudy night, I would not have been able to see them at all were it not for the nearing streetlamps. The light flashed across my face, strobed as it was by the tall grass in a way like quickly waving fingers in front of your eyes. The prairie was giving way to light as I neared the apartments. Brightness grew, but never stopped flashing. It got more yellow too. More colors when I broke through the final grasses and onto a manicured lawn. The brick red of the apartments. Silvers and whites of the cars. Black, puddled asphalt. Light flashed on all surfaces, on me. The side of the parking lot was empty except for me and the flashing. James must have already been almost home, and, like everyone else living there, not outside in the rain. My head buzzed, I was dizzy and short of breath. The flickering light added more colors, blues and reds that glazed in alternating wetted sheets across everything as I rounded the corner of the apartment building and into James' courtyard.

And just like that, I wasn't alone.

It's hard to see when you're confronted with possibilities you've never imagined. I had shown myself to James, exhibited a vision of myself that my friend had never considered, never known to consider. He must have thought that never-boy meant never-friend. He must have thought we'd have to start again, that maybe we'd never started, that I had removed the summer and replaced it with a terror from which to escape. When he ran, he ran not just from me, he also ran back home. Somewhere where the problems were more familiar, more imaginable.

I had imagined too. As I hurtled through the prairie, thoughts were like limbs, pulling through the tall, wet grass. All parts of my actions mirrored in a singular goal. I ran, envisioning catching James, telling him I am the same new person, that a boy and a girl could be friends, as we indeed were. I thought I could get him to hear me. He could listen. We'd be.

That pull of my imagination was strong. It pulled me through the mud and the grass, into the lamplight and around the corner of the apartment complex, and finally into my unimaginable.

Blue and red pulses like the brightest mornings awoke me from dreaming. Atmosphere slowed and physical reality skipped sluggishly back and forth in the alternating light. Police cars. Police too, more than I'd ever seen before, even on the evening news when covering events great and tragic.

I felt as a child sent small. A mass of officers busying at seemingly every corner of the courtyard. They gathered in twos and threes. Doing what, I hadn't a clue. No James. I scanned for the familiar, attempting to push my vision through the rain and the unknown to something I could recognize, as if, in finding that something, I would return to reality.

But I was already there.

I heard a cough as a hand touched my shoulder. It felt cold through the pink translucence of my shirt. I was not startled and let the touch linger. There was a soft and lengthy inhale.

"You okay?" It was Mr. Witmeyer. He exhaled, I smelled no cigarettes, despite his other hand holding one above my face. Another part of me had stopped working.

"Yeah, I think so," my eyes strained.

"Yeah?" He took a drag of his cigarette, half its life obscured by the police lights. "Tough, huh?"

I looked up at him. Several other tenants stood nearby, under an awning, or not, watching the scene.

"I mean, you know, over there," his chin directed me.

"I'm not sure. What's going on?"

"You don't know? You're all wet. I thought, maybe, you'd been watching."

"No."

"Well, something's happened and…"

"Where's James?" I interrupted. I didn't really care what had happened. I just wanted to find my friend, to tell him I was sorry.

"He's there too, but you shouldn't go. Stay here 'til your parents come to get you."

I walked away from Mr. Witmeyer, searching, where his chin gestured, for James. I didn't recognize anything, not a brick, not even my bare feet as they plodded through the colored puddles. It didn't feel like walking, more like gliding on warm, rough ice, or the gentle opening of new wounds. An extraordinary shadow play unfolded before me.

Porch lights and house lamps backlit a stage set for me, a viewer unprepared, at angles and dramas too high and incomprehensible for six-year-old eyes. Seemingly for my confusion, dark, gangling figures policed a courtyard with which I should have been more familiar. I was not and all my motions were slowly driven towards searching for something, anything I would know, could know. I became aware that the shadowy figures were searching for something too, but they moved more methodically than I, their action practiced.

I hadn't yet caught my breath from my chase to catch James and I was suddenly aware of my exhaustion, as if it had only, just then, caught up with me. My breathing became paced as I crossed the parking lot. The shadows grew flesh and clothing as I neared. Badges and guns soon beamed dangerous blue and red edges. Everything played out before me should have been more terrifying, but my desire to find James, my need to rectify our friendship in that moment mattered more. "I see no short shadows, so James must have made it through all this," I thought. "He must have. He's probably in his apartment already."

I became more determined to find him, as if my survival depended on his affirmations. Amongst the shadows, it was not enough to recognize myself. I wished James to know me.

And if he could not, no one might ever know me.

I might be wrong. I might be alone. It just couldn't be true. I sensed there was no one else like me; James was supposed to have remained. Instead, I felt adrift. Alone. Untethered and I would not last.

My eyes pushed past the shadows and I saw that James' door was open. "He must have been in a hurry," I thought. "His mom'll be pissed!"

I imagined James' muddy, bare footprints tracing through the entryway, up the stairs, down the hall, and into his bedroom. His mom would soon have found them, ten-toed stains on the carpet, a memory of our falling away. She'd turn her ire and attention from James' sister onto him, yelling and pitching his things down the stairs.

She'd told him to wear his shoes, to be smart. All his broken toys would be his fault. And James, released from the safety of our friendship and thrown into his mother's rage, would respond. He was old enough to decide when to wear his shoes. He was smart, smarter than her, and the broken toys, everything would be her fault. His sister would begin to cry, then be shut in her room, leaving her to wait until their mother had finished with James. Maybe the erupting anger wouldn't last long. Maybe the activity of the police outside, in their own drama, would serve to distract and pacify, or at least delay the inevitable. Perhaps time would sooth the coming pains, regrets, grief. I didn't want anyone to be hurt, least of all James. I could still stop it. I could apologize, let them know that everyone was blameless except for me.

I indicted myself in a racing negotiation that ran in my head as fast as I was running towards the apartments. The muddy footprints became mine as I seized on the idea that everything that was about to happen, was happening, would not have happened were it not for my insistence that we go to the prairie in the first place, as if one thing necessarily follows the other. I believed these collapsing increments, these causes and effects, to center around me, devoid of the possibility that every other moment or action might also have played their part. Consequences are more concentric and nebulous than to be singularly centering. They are overlapping and hard to pin down. Where was the blame has always been the wrong question as it is a question alone and apart. But I was differently foolish then.

James' sister's sickness became mine too, and his mother's anger, and his revulsion. I would take it all in if it would mean they were okay. I would apologize for anything and everything if I could get one last friendly embrace, or even a momentary exchange of acknowledging glances, just enough of a look through the tears to accept and ending. To be safe, I would say goodbye.

I would not get a chance.

I was clotheslined back to reality about halfway to James' door. An officer's arm reached out and stopped me, though my breath and sight still raced forward, searching for James. The officer's arm was drier than mine, stiff and inflexible. My pink shirt clung partway around his jacket, as if it too was trying to reach James. I relented, wet and sobbing. The officer began talking, but my hearing was nowhere.

An ambulance pulled out in front of us, quiet and slow.

Then a police car, a woman in the back I couldn't quite recognize through all the blinking water.

And there he was, James, sitting in the front passenger's seat of an open police cruiser. Someone had put a police jacket on him and an officer was handing him a paper cup of something steamy. He never looked over, and when I yelled to him, it was on the inside, audible only to me.

He didn't look like he was there and had been rendered small, a distant being, cold, wet, and alone.

A solitary blinker. Just like me.

Summer

Hutchinson, KS

KALENE NISLY

I'm 31 years old. This is the summer I came out. This is the summer I fell in love. This is the summer my house got painted.

This is the summer the paint got chipped away to make way for the new. The cicadas died, white bellies exposed to the sky. Now I understand their vulnerability. I do not relish their destruction.

"It's complicated." We've all said it so many times. "This is complicated." It is an answer; it is a question. We whisper it to ourselves, "Literally nothing is strange anymore," which means, eventually, that everything is. And we are learning to accept this fact. We lean forward and somehow it feels as if we are learning backwards.

This is the summer I walked in a river at sunrise, but I still stood in the dark. We didn't know much then. This is still true. Sometimes, when the wind is just right, it can look like the river is flowing backwards. I understand something about this. I feel it in myself.

Summer is ending. The hills are covered in the colors of it. I'm jealous of the certainty of their blush. Mine is still so quick to come, so out of my control. I'm learning to surrender to it.

Summer is ending. The house is nearly painted. The conversations that leave me standing, exposed and skinless, praying for protection, are nearly over.

This is the summer I fell in love. This is the summer, that like the cicadas, I came out. This is the summer that like the river, I learned not everything is as it seems. And like the river, I can't stop spilling over.

This is the summer I fell in love.

Fickle, Inexplicable

Columbus, OH

JACKIE HEDEMAN

The summer I started eating green bell peppers, I was looking for a job. The hunger came on suddenly with the June humidity. I wanted something fresh to hold me up, to keep me open. I was as energetic as a coiled spring, walking miles along the eastern edge of Columbus every evening with earbuds and podcasts. Not yet brave enough to patio-dine alone, I poured a glass of rosé into a transparent blue water bottle (free, one Sunday mass; "Our Lady of Victory" and a white cross affixed) and carried it with me, chasing the scent of backyard grilling through the affluent neighborhood near my apartment.

It was a summer of waiting. After three years in Columbus in an MFA program, I was applying to jobs all across the country. I had to be ready to move at a moment's notice, I reasoned, so I made very few plans. Ordinary days accelerated from leisurely breakfast (Honey Nut Cheerios and a mug of black tea) to hours of job search and applications, conducted, more often than not, at an underappreciated suburban coffee shop where the chairs pressed crosshatch patterns into my bare thighs. My beverage of choice for the job hunt was iced green tea; anything more caffeinated and my entire core would clench into an anxious fist.

That summer, I learned that green bell peppers are unripe. I wondered by whose definition they were unripe. Green peppers were harvested and eaten. Cut up into strips and refrigerated. Brought out of the refrigerator and snacked on like chips. I had never enjoyed fruit for dessert or vegetables for snack. Who was I suddenly?

It was because they tasted like cold water.

I drove across fields up to Ann Arbor to visit my friend Katy, a woman who has insisted at various points in our ten plus year friendship that she does not have her life together. And that might very well be the case—I have learned to believe people when they say this because appearance is hardly ever reality—but Katy eats three square meals a day, kayaks the Huron River, joins clubs to make friends, and avoids YouTube spirals so comprehensively that she has no clue who or what YouTubers are.

On my visit, we sat on her porch after dark and under the cicada hum I tried to tell her some things that I was about to share in wide-release. She wasn't on social media; she wouldn't see my passive coming out announcement. She wouldn't learn I was queer unless I told her. So I told her, only I told her in the context of a two-person truth or dare game, the kind fueled by wine where every dare becomes a truth and both people answer each question for the fun of it.

I knew an opening would come, and eventually Katy asked, "Are there any of your friends you couldn't see yourself dating?"

I considered, though I knew the answer almost immediately. "A couple," I said. "But not because they're not men."

Katy didn't seem surprised. I tried to remember whether I'd already told her in a different way, or whether she'd just felt it in everything I'd ever written. Maybe she was surprised and I just couldn't read her face in the dark. Her streetlamp was burned out; the most reliable light source came from passing headlights, barreling down to the Broadway Street bridge.

I kept a list, in those days, of the people I told. Katy was sandwiched high up on the list between my parents and my therapist. She doesn't know it, but coming out to her, feet up and swatting mosquitos, was the easiest coming out of my life.

Something like irresponsibility

I-71

HARMONY COX

In the months before I came out of the closet and asked my husband for a separation, I did a lot of things. I googled terms like "later-in-life lesbian" and "irreconcilable differences." I quietly began the work of separating our finances. I slept in my bed—my newly-purchased separate bed, where I'd been sleeping while we tried to work things out—felt the cold space next to me, and cried.

But mostly, I drove.

Ohio is my home state, the place where I have lived most of my life. I suspect there might be something uniquely Ohioan about being soothed by the highway.

In 1984, the year I was born, the Ohio Division of Transit and Tourism came up with a new slogan to explain our state to the rest of the country: "Ohio, The Heart of It All."—ostensibly because Ohio is kind of shaped like a heart, if you squint at a map of the United States and don't know much about anatomy. And thus if Ohio is the heart of it all, the chambers are made by the vascular divisions of its interstates. Vehicles are the blood cells of Ohio, carrying people to their intended destinations swiftly and safely. To occupy one of these cells, to be in transit, is one of my favorite things to do.

Every distance in Ohio is not measured in feet or miles, but minutes spent driving to your destination. If you hop on I-71, you can drive Ohio's tip to tail in just about six hours. I-70 will take you east to west, Indiana to West Virginia, in about the same amount of time. My favorite, I-270, is known as the Outerbelt. It takes you on a neat, never ending circular tour of Columbus and its many suburbs. I live on the city side, where the curves glide you past the tiny, glittering skyscrapers of our old-fashioned downtown.

Driving these highways is a practical way to get around, but it's also a way to get your head straight. I would make up some excuse to get myself out of the house and spend hours in the darkness, circling Columbus with a pack of cigarettes and a massive Sonic lemonade. I'd lose myself in the meditative hum of wheels on asphalt, counting the numbers on the exits and letting the high-beams distract me from my tears.

I'd been through three therapists in ten years, each of whom had their own exit on this highway. The Lane Avenue exit led to the university hospital, where I'd gone in graduate school to see a therapist for help in sorting out my pre-wedding anxieties. He listened patiently for twenty minutes, then he told me I had to call it off because he'd never known a queer woman to stay happily married to a straight man. I didn't have the courage to question him, so I let myself believe my growing discomfort with my impending matrimony was my own fault, because I was too queer to be a good wife. So I put my queerness aside, and refused to think about it for a long time.

Another exit, this one to Granville. Where I sought out therapy again, this time when a close relationship with a friend became confusing. She had found a new boyfriend, and I was experiencing a sharp and painful jealousy that I didn't have the context to understand.

(But the highway does; there, the exit that leads to the favorite restaurant where she held my hand and told me I was the most important person in her world. There, the exit to the bus station where she wept as she kissed me goodbye! The only thing she needed more than me was to stay in her comfort zone, so you can guess why we parted ways in the end.)

After I described my plight, my new therapist leaned forward with a confused look on his face.

"But if you think you're bisexual, how do you know if you're in love with a friend or you just care about them a lot?"

I stared at him, biting back the sting of tears. "I don't know. That's why I'm seeing you."

It was the third therapist, off the exit to Upper Arlington, who actually understood. She was a specialist in LGBTQ identity issues, and she helped me untangle my confusion and jealousy and set me on the right path. She forced me to acknowledge the truth: that I was a closeted queer woman, that I was deeply unhappy as a result, and that as much as I loved my husband I could not be the wife he needed me to be. That was when I realized I would have to eventually set out alone, away from the man who I thought

I'd be spending the rest of my life with. This journey, like my endless looping trips on the highway, could only be my own.

Realizing it was one thing. Accepting it was something else entirely.

I had already been testing our boundaries, but I didn't cheat on him. We even had an grudgingly open relationship towards the end, when we were trying to figure out if we could possibly stay together. It didn't matter. I knew he resented me for it, and I still felt unfaithful to him. I was the one who was going out by myself to flirt with women. I never actively courted their attention, but I never did anything to dissuade them when they clocked me and complimented my leather jackets and bought me drinks.

I never went home with them either; I'd always make some excuse, an early day at work or feeling a bit under the weather, and I'd leave before they'd think to ask for my number. Just a few minutes spent on vacation from my straight life, then back in the car. It is an easy jump from the brewery district to the highway interchange. I would be back on the road before I realized what I was driving away from. However, I never went home, not right away.

Instead, I drove.

As I drove, I'd feel my body drift with the curve of the highway, my head gently bobbing from left to right. I'd count off the exits to the suburbs. The Easton condos. Westerville. Hilliard, and beyond that, Gahanna. These were the places that had sprawled into clusters of McMansions during the Columbus population boom of the mid-2000s. Acres of forests and farmlands, obliterated and replaced with cheesy-sounding gated communities meant to honor the things that had been sacrificed to create them. The Ravine at Scioto. Farmer's Street. The Residency at Creekside.

The prevalence of gigantic single-family homes in Columbus is both environmentally irresponsible and morally obscene; it's the definition of sprawl and waste. But developers built these places because in my town there is a thirst for this American dream. Sometimes it seems like everyone I know is moving out of the city, away from the bustle and fun of happy hours and into the "starter houses" that will shelter the families they're ready to bring into being. The toy doll pairings of my coupled friends, taking the next step.

When I drove by these exits, I would think of the people who lived there. People I knew, people who were also married, people who embraced a fate that seemed worse than death to me. I'd imagine these people seated at the Target tables in their IKEA kitchens, sorted neatly into houses with the exact same floor plan, each house's vinyl siding a complementary shade of pale pink or blue. Happy with the life they'd chosen.

I would cry and ask myself what was wrong with me, what was broken in me that made me want something else. Why imagining leaving my metro lifestyle behind for the sake of a school district made me want to drive my car off the side of the road and into a telephone pole. I'd try to picture myself with a baby in my arms, a man by my side, but all I could see was static.

When I got tired of listening to myself cry, I'd turn on the radio. Singing along with a car stereo is the cheapest and most readily available form of therapy that Midwesterners are willing to accept. People might think it odd if you sit in a small room with a stranger and try to draw lines between your ugly past and your current neuroses, but nobody will look twice if you spend a few minutes howling along to Journey's greatest hits while stuck in the I-161 traffic circle clusterfuck.

My favorite band to listen to during these late-night drives was Against Me!, a punk band I'd kind of liked in high school but rediscovered with a vengeance during this time of woe. There was one particular song that I liked to sing along with: "Pretty Girls (The Mover)," off of the album *Searching for a Former Clarity*. It's a song written by Laura Jane Grace about the pieces of herself that ended relationships with women before they could begin, and her fear that nobody (including herself) can accept her for who she really is:

And if she says yes, know what intentions might be
If one thing leads to another and there's some chemistry
You cannot lie, you have to tell the truth
You have to explain why this could never be
Cause there are things that cannot be undone
There are mistakes that will never be forgiven
Sometimes at night, I pray to wake
A different person in a different place
I just want to be young, I want to live
God, I want to be healthy, I don't want this problem
You wouldn't think something like irresponsibility
Would complicate something like asking for some company

But there are things you must accept as said and done
There are truths you must learn to confront
You can pray all night and day
You'll always wake the same person in the same place

It's a sad and anxious song, and I felt it in my bones every time it came on. I'd sing aloud with it loudly, freely weeping, taking comfort in the misery I shared with Grace. Sometimes I would put it on repeat, and let it loop around me the same way I endlessly looped around my city in the night.

One night I accidently put on the live recording of the song instead of the studio version. I was surprised to learn that the lyrics had changed since it was first recorded. When Searching for a Former Clarity was released, Laura Jane Grace had not come out as transgender yet. She was still grappling with that realization and what it meant for her, and she wasn't ready to share it. So she'd selectively censored some of the lyrics to the songs she wrote about it. In this particular song, she'd used "irresponsibility" instead of "gender identity" for the studio recording. The live recording gave it the context and meaning it was intended to have.

The true meaning of the song hit me like a slap. Of course, the song was about being closeted and the way it isolates you from other people. No wonder I felt so connected to it, even before I knew what it was about. I don't mean to conflate my journey with that of Grace's, or borrow the pain of transgender individuals to make a point about my own sexuality. But the ache of hiding yourself from the world for so long, and the grinding pain of working so hard to avoid your own truth, is a theme that could not help but resonate with me in that moment. It felt like the song had come to me before I'd realized how much I needed it, in a disguise so I'd receive the message without overthinking it. Only now did I understand what the lyrics really meant, and why they made me sob into my lemonade.

As Grace wisely notes, there are truths you must learn to confront. A punk song may not be the ideal cardinal north for a journey into a new world, but I could not deny that hiding who I was and what I wanted was crushing me, and that sustaining a marriage on the back of my pain wasn't going to work forever. I had to stop running from the truth. No matter how much therapy I underwent, no matter how I prayed or pleaded for something else, I would always be the same person at the end of the day. And that person didn't want to be married, and wasn't particularly attracted to cisgender men, and had never let herself live openly as a queer person before. There was a whole new future before me, so much unexplored possibility if I just stopped driving in the same circles and let myself consider a different path. I deserved to be happy in a way the exits to the suburbs never could provide. I was always meant to keep moving.

So I told my husband the truth, we recognized our differences were irreconcilable, and we split up. I remained in my hometown, determined to chase my own happiness until I found it. All I had to do was end my marriage of a decade, come out to my friends and family, and learn how to be queer at the tender young age of thirty-five. Not an easy journey to start, but at least I was finally ready to begin.

pink_sissy

St. Louis, MO

JOSS BARTON

A photo of pink_sissy when she wasn't looking: bitch had just started 'mones and her hair was wrapped in silk mod pattern scarf, posted on IG and child, she reads me in the name of Lazarus, said she was taking out the trash like the fleets in my waste can, like the anon cum loads oozing out my ass.

The word Ode feels too soft for the cocks she memorized in type font Craigslist ads plastered along South Grand-left on Chippewa-swerve on a tranny memory-take a left at the cursed intersection at Gustine where cars & pickup trucks full of beer soaked day laborers meet in glass ridden amazement-roll past the flats of immigrants growing young peppers in front lawn gardens and ruddish women woven in rainbow cloth on stoops-readjust a chubby cock in mesh basketball shorts as you park the HONDA-pass through the storm door-

KNOCK TWICE-
ASK IF TRANSSEXUAL DYSTOPIA IS HOME-
ASK IF ALL THE FULLY FUNCTIONAL TRANNY TOPS HAVE
MOVED TO CLEVELAND-
ASK IF WE WERE ABANDONED BY THE ANAL SEX GODS
WHOSE PUNISHMENT ARE MEN WHO DON'T RIM!
    HOLY MOTHERS! PROTECT US IN THIS TIME OF
    HOMOSEXUAL BANALITY!
    DO NOT TRUST THE GAY WHITE MAN RUNNING FOR
    PRESIDENT!
    DO NOT TRUST CIS SAVIORS!
    DO NOT TRUST WHITE WOMEN WHO DO NOT LISTEN
    TO BLACK WOMEN!
    AND DON'T EVER FUCKING TRUST TRADE WITH YOUR
CAR!   AMERICA! MOTHER OF MULES! QUEEN OF HOLLOW
VIRTUE!

Sing us a song, scratch the bowels and paint flowers with the blood, tell us the world is beautiful, on the other side of barb wire fences, where owls hang, executed by divine destiny. Rip the sheet metal off my back, straddle the bones of my satin bedpost, saturate Saturday sins with seroconversion-sonnets, and pink_sissy crushing a roach beneath concrete bitten pumps, see the guts, white and soft, smell the stink of insect brains wiped across the sole as a site for parasites, the kind of tongue that roots into a man's asshole searching for real lies: static stars in her hair another anointed ass to breed: another question of what it means to be alive in this world, at this time, surrounded by these horrors: another movie to check into the viewing queue: another strain to mutate: another world app fucked and wiped with snot rag cocks slimy and pulsating and her lips whore neon as she enters the temple, stoned, burning the foreheads of faggot elders, pumping her transsexual cock and cumming on the money tables. The boys call it hell, they send her texts of cock pics and coke mirrors begging to breed her, everyone wants a whore, but no one wants to wake up next to one

The problem for many old guard gays is that trannies are now living the lives that dangerous faggots used to live, which in part, produces both jealousy and resentment, that the dolls are more subversive more radical more gorgeous and more cock hungry than they ever were, SO IT IS WHAT IS ALWAYS IS: TRANS MISOGYNY FROM BITTER QUEENS: How fucking typical it is that right now its trans women of color, BLACK AND BROWN TRANS WOMEN, who must grin until our lips bleed as we watch our rainbow peers pat themselves on the backs for their tranny flag avatars while simultaneously refusing to radically and fiercely protect and nourish us: We get to see how much our lives really mean as we count the hashtags against the job offers, the HIV infections against the second/third/fourth/fifth chances, the willingness to let us bleed out our political traumas on stages and screens for THEIR HEALING against the bruises on our bodies and the obituaries they never read.

pink_sissy sheds the skin off her nipples like human scales, wraps her heart together with a bouquet of transsexual molting, bites the flesh, rips the ligament memories, warms a nest of cellophane with the light of electricity against a black sky stabbed with white pins poked through the lining of night silk. Haunted bodies buried beneath this estrogen soaked skin brittle nails chipped on the teeth of transsexual ghosts wailing for freedom or a chance to try it over again to re-wind the tape and roll the dice and this time aim for healing or heaven or anywhere but eternally stuck on this elevator to Human Resources.

She keeps trying to write something better than these tranny Pornhub poems, she sits down to type a title: NO MORE DEATH POEMS: tries to find sentences symbolism stanzas about absolutely anything: rows of lines on watermelon seeds spit from the wet pink lips of milkweed boys smoking pot in red florescent bar lights: prose on detective Pikachu, pisco sours, pine trees in June, potted plants in macrame webs: Haikus on the Holy Trans Mothers: Sylvia Sylvester Marsha Ms. Major Ms. Leon TS Madison Tracey Norman Candis Cayne Candy Darling CeCe McDonald Crystal LeBeija Laverne Cox Trace Lysette Flawless Sabrina Van Barnes Bamby Salcedo Maria Roman Passion Principle Janet Mock: BUT ALL THAT COMES OUT ARE THE AGES AND NAMES AND HOMETOWNS AND NAMES AND CAUSES OF DEATH AND THE NAMES AND OCCUPATIONS AND THE FUCKING NAMES AND THEIR HOB-BIES AND THEIR FUCKING NAMES and the rhythm of repetition fades into white noise but she thinks, this is what an sounds like, dead static silence running across the black nothingness of Arkansas as she drives out of Memphis. How can anyplace be so pitch black? So empty? No trees or stars or the whir of moths or the screams of locusts or the hoots of owls or the soul catching of whippoorwills or the howls of coyotes or the chirps of rain frogs? Every rattle and bump on this goddamn road reminds her how fucked she will be if she breaks down here. She left the last gas station a good hour ago, and there's only the white eyes of a semi-truck in the deso-late distance floating in more darkness ahead of her, and a crackling voice across the radio relays a message that catastrophic tornadoes have ripped across Missouri. The sky blinks in balmy storm lights against other kinds of veins. pink_sissy sips on stale coffee as she continues driving through the night, until she reaches the dull haze of Saint Louis.

I've Got a Hard-On for Jesus

Chicago, IL

ELIZABETH HARPER

I've got a hard-on for Jesus.

Early, early on in my childhood
psychosexual development,
before Shaun Cassidy
and John Travolta,
even before Davy Jones and
wanting to be a live-in
housekeeper/ sex-slave
for all The Monkees,
there was Jesus.

He looked so cool in the pictures
with his long chestnut hair and beard.
And he was such a genuinely nice guy, too.
The first famous anarchist-feminist,
yet so misunderstood.
And who wouldn't go for a guy
helpless and pinned to a cross.
S & M, here I come.
Hey Jesus, I'll wash your feet,
and suck your cock, too!

Jesus Christ Superstar and *Godspell*
are my porn. I could come watching
a 20-something Victor Garber
dancing around and singing
in a Superman t-shirt.

I would get up early
to go to Sunday school,
even in the coldest Chicago winters,
and my daddy would take me,

so I could learn about Jesus and
read the bible and write poems and
do projects in papier-mâché.

I'd fantasize about meeting Jesus
in real life on the street.
I'd invite him in to have hot chocolate and
John's frozen cheese pizzas.
I really thought this could happen
since Jesus looked a lot like the guys on Clark street
my dad would point out to me as heroin addicts.
But this worried me, too.
What if my folks wouldn't let Jesus come over
because they thought he was a long-haired, hippie,
freaked-out heroin addict?
I was really worried I would come across Jesus
and he would be turned away.
Especially since I knew we were soul mates
and I really understood Jesus and
we were destined to be together forever and
just the thought of him made me feel all tingly
in my special place in my underpants.

This was probably the beginning of my realization
that adults were hypocritical liars
with reputations and property to protect.
They didn't really want me fucking Jesus,
even if, in a way, they said they did.

Jesus loves me!
The bible tells me so!
He loves all the little children!
I love Jesus!
The bible tells me to!
I want him inside me!
So I'll never be alone!

"I've Got a Hard-On for Jesus" first appeared in *Friction,* an issue of *Children, Churches, and Daddies* from Scars Publications

Long Distance

Central Illinois

ROBYN STEELY

A few months into the relationship—not quite the beginning but too far in for me to run—she told me about the time she smashed beer bottles on concrete and rubbed her hands in the glass. She made a movie in my head, a montage of taut pink palms, chunks of brown glass, and shiny gold bits of Michelob labels. I pictured it at night because who would do such a thing in daylight? Maybe it didn't happen this way, but I imagined her hands meeting glass on the short stoop out back of her cheap off-campus rental. I thought about the rusty screen door that led out to the stoop, and the crumbled concrete steps littered with cigarette butts and the terrible clues she left for her roommate to find the next morning.

As she told me about the beer bottles and her hands, she never mentioned blood, and I never thought about blood or bloodiness. As she spoke, her eyes were fiercely brown, black really—a darkness that often unsteadied me, especially in that moment. The whites were so white, almost like ping pong balls. I worried they might pop right out of her head. For a moment, I wanted them to. Because then she would be a cartoon character. In a cartoon, she would magically come back together, unscathed. What she was telling me would be a fantasy, made up. A story.

But it wasn't a story. It was her life, handed to me, and she wanted me to do something with it. I gave her some calm, understanding words in return before filing her misdirected brutality away. We dated for a while after that, but neither of us brought it up again. I've thought about her over the years, of course, and all those miles I drove on I-70 to see her. Even now, sometimes in the summer, when I push open a screen door, I press my fingers hard against the tight gridded metal. When the hinges creak, I remember her hands, her small perfect hands, and how ruthless they were.

'does she mind'

St. Louis, MO

ANONYMOUS

She said, *I love you so much*
I say she cares too much.

She keeps me around,
Though I don't trust much.

Sometimes we hold hands;
It's new. I don't touch much.

Lately, my brain keeps saying,
Use her as crutch, much?

But she's my girl, the best girl.
We used to double-dutch.

So when she says, *I love you*
I smile and say, *How much?*

She looks to me, not smiling,
Before she says, *Too much.*

When I'm With Her / Pua Yog Koj

A reprise of WOMN + WOMN, *a musical*

St. Paul, MN

KA "OSKAR" LY

When I'm with her, I'm an artist
I am free, I am whole
I am light, I am alive
I have wings
I have so much to give

It's getting blurry
I'm losing
My imagination
Caught up in the window
Of this reality

I struggle
Going·on and on
In circles, everyday
In my dreams, living
Our happiness

Pua yog koj	(Is it you?)
Zoo lis koj lub suab	(Sounds of your voice)
Pua yog koj	(Is it you?)
Zoo lis yus npau suav	(Like in a dream)
Koj pua nco ub cog lus	(Do you remember our promise?)
Pua tseem nco yav tag lo	(Remember the days?)
Pua tseem muaj ib los lus	(Do you still have a word?)
Zoo rau kuv... los rau ub	(Kind words for me... for us)
Kuv quaj los	(I cry, despite)
Kua muag tsis los	(No tears falling)
Kuv quaj los	(I cry, despite)

Koj yuav tsis hnov   (You won't hear it)
Kuv quaj los   (I cry, despite)
Lub suab tsis nrov   (The voice of no sound)
Kuv quaj los   (I cry, despite)
Tsis muaj kua muag   (There'll be no tears)

Arch

Watersmeet, MI

K. ANN MACNEIL

What I miss most about being with you involves squeezing into Three Lives & Company (after I have to ask myself if it's on West 10th or West 11th) without having to worry about making chat.

It's about being sure that I'm there to look at books, and to think about books, and to buy books, even, (after I have to ask myself if it's toward or away from West 4th), not to have to decide if I want to be introduced to a very gay poet of some very small, very recent note.

It's about cashmere and caramels wrapped in wax paper that you made with your mother in her kitchen on the lake, about the way you asked me to pick and meant it, about a square silver ring, charmed or not, with a date inside that was a promise to myself that slipped off of my finger in a woozy arch, and through the gaps in porch floorboards, outside Watersmeet (Michigan or Wisconsin, I forget) the minute I had kept it, before even I realized.

Sonic Healing in St. Louis

St. Louis, MO

SYLVIA SUKOP

At the Center for Hearing and Speech, a St. Louis audiology clinic, Dr. Koach Baruch Frazier wears a blue lab coat and, low on his left lapel, a small pin—a close-up image of an ear. The ear on the pin is a shade of brown resembling Frazier's own skin tone and, until I pointed it out to him, he did not realize he had placed it on his heart.

Listening with the heart is one side of a sonic equation that has defined Frazier's life. As the Center's chief of audiology, he sees hundreds of patients a year at two different clinic locations, one in a well-to-do, mostly white southern suburb of St. Louis, and one in a majority African American neighborhood on the low-income north side. In this divided city, the doctor is known for his gentle manner and ability to forge compassionate relationships with patients across a broad spectrum of backgrounds and needs.

In over a decade of practice, Frazier, who is in his late thirties, has seen all the ways that difficulty hearing can lead to debilitating social isolation and diminished quality of life. It's what first drew him to this work, seeking to help a family friend, a military veteran with Ménière's disease, which affected her inner ear, causing vertigo, tinnitus, and gradual hearing loss. He changed his major at St. Louis University from pre-med to audiology, and went on to earn a doctorate in audiology at Central Michigan University.

"Addressing hearing impairment," he says, "is about reconnecting people to their lives."

He never rushes patient visits and simply by decelerating, sitting with them, and listening to their stories, he can discern challenges they face (ranging from family and workplace to financial and spiritual) that go beyond the immediate hearing or speech problem that first brought them to his office, allowing him to make an even bigger impact on their quality of life.

In settings far removed from the hushed and sterile space of the clinic, with its high-tech medical equipment and one-on-one meetings by appointment, a different but equally vital aspect of Frazier's sonic identity finds expression. Playing a large Djembe drum strapped to his five-foot-five frame, the percussionist and singer has been at the center of major protest marches from the streets of Ferguson to downtown St. Louis. A longtime racial justice and LGBTQIA* activist, he has a gift for channeling the often volatile energy of a public demonstration into resolutely nonviolent collective chanting. His instrument, a West African-style, rope-tuned, goatskin-head drum, takes its name from a saying of the Bambara people in Mali: *Anke djé, anke bé,* or "everyone gather together in peace."

In the sanctuary

Frazier also plays the Djembe in religious settings, including every Friday night at Central Reform Congregation (CRC) in St. Louis's Central West End, where he serves as a cantorial soloist and song leader. It was in CRC's bright, modern sanctuary that I first encountered Frazier in the summer of 2016, drumming and singing on the *bima* (altar), wearing a *kippa* (yarmulke), *tzitzit* (long white tassels or ritual fringes that hang out from under a shirt), and a large, black leather pendant with a gold-colored Lion of Judah mounted on a Star of David in the colors of the Pan-African flag (horizontal bands of red, black, and green). A composer and liturgical innovator, he is known for blending music from different traditions while making it accessible to everyone.

Frazier's signature repertoire includes several such prayer-song mash-ups, one of which weaves the Shaker hymn "Sanctuary" (O Lord prepare me / to be a sanctuary / pure and holy / tried and true / With thanksgiving / I'll be a living / sanctuary for you) together with the Hebrew liturgical prayer from Psalm 51 (*Adonai s'fatai tiftach ufi yagid t'hilatecha,* translating to "Eternal God, open up my lips that my mouth may declare Your praise"). The significance of both prayers, and one reason they pair so well, is that each emphasizes the body, one's human agency and utterances, as the place where God dwells. Both lyrics speak from an "I" voice—a direct and individual relationship with God.

While the lyrics are important and inspiring, the melody is perhaps even more crucial, the "carrier" that brings all the voices in the room together. Frazier always opens with a *nigun,* a wordless melody that can be sung on any syllable (such as *na na na* or *yai dai dai*) or simply hummed along to. It's the easy on-ramp by which anyone can enter. The song then proceeds with a we're-in-no-hurry quality that helps elongate this moment of entry into the central prayer that follows, the *Amidah* (or standing prayer), at which point the words shift from the first-person singular "I" into the plural "we" as congregants make the transition from individuals into a community.

A newcomer to St. Louis, I had been *shul* shopping and figured it would take time to find a community that felt as *heymish* (homey) to me as the one I had just left after two decades in Los Angeles. That community, Beth Chayim Chadashim (House of New Life), had the historical distinction of being the world's first gay and lesbian synagogue, founded in 1972 in the early days of the gay liberation movement. I soon learned that, like me, Frazier grew up Christian and, while committed to a life of God-centered community, the one he was born into was not the one he felt he ultimately belonged to. Both of us would find our true spiritual home in Reform Judaism.

Frazier's identity as a trans man was not merely a known fact at CRC (with its majority white, heterosexual membership) but was communally embraced and even celebrated. The entire congregation knew that Frazier would be undergoing top surgery in the fall, just ahead of Rosh Hashanah (the Jewish new year), and that he would celebrate his *barbat mitzvah* the following spring. (Frazier made the unusual decision to maintain the referents to both genders in the ritual's title, *bar* for male and *bat* for female, and not to separate them, even with a hyphen.) Coming into his authentic identities has been a long process, but one he feels was destined: "I really believe I always have been a Jew, I just didn't have any words to describe it. Like I've always been trans, I didn't know what to call being trans. I knew that I was this thing different from everyone else around me but I didn't know what to call it."

In the various spaces he inhabits, from the clinic to the sanctuary to the streets, Frazier is routinely confronted by questions, curious looks, and outright discrimination. But it is through voice—his own and that of others—that he navigates and shapes his daily experience and impact in the world.

Frazier discovered his sonic calling growing up in an extended family of African Methodist Episcopal ministers, including his grandfather Jesse Peterson Sr., his uncle Jesse Peterson Jr., his aunt Mandella, and her husband Johnnie, who, along with Frazier's mother, all grew up in Okeechobee, Florida. His mother has always been a church singer, and Frazier joined the choir at age five or six. He and his parents would travel to Florida from their home in Kansas City, Missouri, for large family reunions, and the power of their communal singing was, he says, always "something to behold."

The family's most beloved song is an 18th-century Methodist hymn, "A charge to keep I have, a God to glorify." For our first interview, I sat down with Frazier at the men's rooming house where he lives just a block from

CRC synagogue, and sitting beside me at the cluttered table in his shared dining room, two old refrigerators whirring nearby, he intoned the long, drawn-out syllables (a vocal technique known as melisma) of "A charge to keep I have, a God to glorify," tilting his head back, beaming with pleasure at the memory. "What was always so magical to me is that all of us kids, we wouldn't even know what was going on, and all of a sudden you'd hear Granny moaning in the background, and you'd be like, *What is happening?!* Then the energy would go from person to person to person," he recalls, as other family members chimed in, until a great chorus of voices would sustain the vibrational energy, with no fixed end in sight. How long would they go on?, I ask. "Forever," Frazier smiles.

A hallmark of "A charge to keep I have" is the hymn-singing style known as "lining" that dates back to the slavery era in the South. Although enslaved persons were sometimes allowed to attend church, seated in separate sections, most could not read, and so a song leader would sing out lines from the hymnal for the congregation to repeat. To this day, Frazier's family performs this tradition whenever they gather for reunions, and in years past he always marveled at his grandfather's quiet capacity to "manage" the dynamic sonic energy. Witnessing this phenomenon in his family and at church would spark Frazier's future commitment to what he now calls "energy work."

In the streets

People tend to think of sound as immaterial, as something that floats invisibly through the air without physical presence. But researchers who study sound have long recognized its physical properties, without which we would not be able to hear it. Our bodies are designed to receive sound, especially (but not exclusively) our eardrums that transmit sound vibrations from the air to the ossicle bones in the middle ear, and from there to the inner ear's fluid-filled cochlea. Vibration in air is thus converted to vibration in fluid. Sound enters the body; we "contain" it.

But in Frazier's experience, sound also has the capacity to contain *us*. When a shared sonic experience is created with intention, such as communal singing or chanting, the vibrational energy can be shaped and guided in order to "hold" a group together. It works through music, through prayer, and also through chanting in a protest context.

I asked Frazier for words he'd use to describe this energy: "It's mostly emotional, it soothes me. It reminds me of my mother—my mother's a singer. And she used to sing us awake." And he begins singing, lifting his face upward, smiling. "'Rise and shine and give God your glory, glory.' That's how we would wake up every day. It's so maternal. When we sing *nigunim* [wordless melodies] it's the same thing. There's this sort of *blanket* of sound that if I allow it, it will hold me and protect me and keep me warm.

When Rev. Traci Blackmon, pastor of Christ the King UCC in Florissant, was organizing the Mother's March for Justice in October 2014, to take place in Clayton, she asked Frazier to lead the gathering with his drum. Frazier had by then become known for his nightly presence on the streets of Ferguson in the wake of Michael Brown's killing two months earlier, on August 9. Recalling Ferguson in those early days, Frazier says that "police had their rifles trained on us from on top of a tank," dogs were brought out, tear gas was launched, and a military-grade sonic weapon known as the LRAD was deployed. In a crowd whose grief and anger was sometimes on the verge of spilling into violence, his drumming helped unite and direct that energy into chants. "People were looking to me to see what I did"—what chants he would offer or echo (e.g., "No justice, no peace"), and which chants he did not support with his beats (e.g., "Fuck the police").

Rev. Blackmon's intention, says Frazier, was for the Mother's March to be silent. "It was almost to be walking around like Joshua," he says, referring to the Biblical scripture in which God instructs Joshua to have the people march in silence around the city of Jericho once each day for six days, and then, after circling it seven times on the seventh day, to sound the trumpets and let loose such mighty shouts that their sonic force would bring the walls down.

Within the silence that Rev. Blackmon envisaged, says Frazier, "she wanted me to drum. Just me. And I remember it was *shabbas*. Here's this black trans Jew leading this group of women who are grieving their children. Mothers who lost their kids to police violence and to other kinds of violence." He shakes his head, seemingly incredulous.

Because some of the marchers were not able to complete more than one circuit, the group stopped at that point and, without prompting, wailing and keening began. "It broke my heart," Frazier says softly, adding that, again, it was sound that held the group in their grief: "It's a container. It's there to allow people to experience. They didn't need words."

What happened that day at the Mother's March echoed a moment from Frazier's childhood that he will never forget. "One of my classmates died very suddenly," he says somberly. "I went to the viewing. I remember the church was empty, just the mother was there. It was an open casket. I was walking back, after giving my condolences. The mother started wailing. I can't imagine what it must be like to look at a casket [containing your child]. The sound of a mother's voice wailing because they lost their kid. How do you not be affected by that? That's what I wish my Jewish family would understand," he says, alluding to the many Jews he knows that have failed to engage with the realities of racial violence in St. Louis and around the country. "You can't unhear that. I can't unhear a mother wailing. If we transplant ourselves back in Germany, in Poland. *That sound,* what do you do with that?"

In the clinic

On the afternoon I visited the Center for Hearing and Speech, I observed Frazier interacting with patients and other staff. One elderly woman with dementia, accompanied by her middle-aged daughter, was returning to have a recently prescribed hearing aid checked. The mother, white-haired and seated in a wheelchair, had bright blue eyes that matched her shirt, and her hearing aid was also blue. Her demeanor was quiet and slightly bemused. Frazier pulled his chair up close to hers and patiently went through a series of questions and small adjustments. He removed her hearing aid to examine it, and before putting it back, demonstrated a quick way to check if the batteries are working: "If you cup [the hearing aid] in your hand and hear that little screech, you'll know it's getting power."

"It's getting *tired*?" the woman asked.

"No, it's getting *power*," said Frazier with a perfectly calibrated loudness that still conveyed kindness. "The battery's getting *power*."

One of Frazier's specialties is fitting people for hearing aids, and the nonprofit clinic provides generous discounts to low-income patients for high-quality devices. It was nearing the end of his workday and Frazier, having seen all of his scheduled patients, offered to screen *my* hearing. I eagerly accepted.

I had noticed the room-within-the-room where the screening is administered. Window panes on two of its walls allow views in and out, but no sound gets through in either direction. Frazier took me inside, and though I worried the booth might feel claustrophobic, it was large enough for several people to stand in. The walls were covered in sound-insulating panels and draped about with bundled wires and cables of different sizes and colors.

He had me sit in the only seat, an old-fashioned armchair with a row of brass rivets edging its leather upholstery. The chair wasn't the only antique in the room: Frazier pulled from a shelf the 1971 edition of a spiral-bound book titled *Word Intelligibility Picture Identification* (WIPI). Based on children's illustrated vocabulary books with a grid of six images to a page, it's a widely used tool to assess a child's speech recognition before they can read. When the audiologist says, *Show me* _____, the child, if they can both hear and understand, points to the image that matches the word spoken. Not surprisingly, the book is a veritable case study of outmoded and racially inscribed representations, depicting, for example, all body parts such as "knee," "thumb," and "neck" as white—indeed, to my eye, as *pink,* which makes these kinds of already abstract images, severed from the body, difficult even for me to decipher with certainty. Later I learn that such problems of "pictorial confusion" and potential test bias in the WIPI has been critiqued by expert practitioners within the field and the book has since been updated. One more visual moment before my screening began: Using an otoscope, an illuminated speculum for the ear, Frazier peered inside my ear canal. "Do you use Q-tips?" he asked. I confessed that I do. "Why do you use them?" Because my ears feel itchy inside, like they need to be cleaned. "*Everybody* thinks they need to use Q-tips," he says, making me feel slightly less guilty, "but no one really needs to. It does more harm than good." Besides interfering with the healthy presence of wax in the ear canal, which helps keep it moist and well-protected, inserting Q-tips risks damaging the ear drum.

Excessive noise can also damage the ear drum. In fact the field of audiology emerged after World War II when many members of the military came back with damaged ears. Loud artillery fire and explosions, and sometimes direct physical injury to the ear, all took their toll, and rehabilitation centers to diagnose and address hearing loss were opened around the country. The standard test to evaluate hearing was conducted on a device known as an audiometer, via which "pure tones" of various frequencies are sounded into each ear and the subject, using a hand signal, indicates when a tone is heard.

Today that testing device is basically the same. Frazier gently places a thin plastic tube in each of my ears—an "insert earphone" as opposed to a headset—and makes sure they feel comfortable to me before he steps out of the booth, closing the door behind him. He takes a seat in front of the audiometer device, at a little desk just outside the window I am facing. I can see him but I cannot hear him until he activates the microphone that transmits his words into the booth.

"OK, so I want you to raise your finger whenever you hear a sound, even if it's very very quiet." The sounds begin, faintly. I sense myself straining to hear them, but I do hear them. It's not an electronic beep but something more subtle, a mere hint of a sound, like one tiny thread

in the dense sonic fabric that I am more accustomed to hearing. I raise my finger many times.

Next, the speech recognition test: In the same way the audiologist uses the "carrier phrase" *Show me* _____ to prompt a child to point to the "target" image, they use the carrier phrase *Say the word* _____ when testing adults, and the subject repeats that word.

Say the word sled. Sled. *Say the word tree.* Tree. *Say the word praise.* Praise. *Say the word mouth.* Mouth. *Say the word hunt.* Hunt. *Say the word box.* Box. *Say the word teach.* Teach. Frazier and I volleyed the words back and forth like this, rhythmically, almost musically, as we went through the long list together. I had the realization that we were enacting the same type of call-and-response that Frazier uses on the streets, leading the crowd in a chant; that he uses in the sanctuary, leading the congregation in prayer-song; and that he uses at his family gatherings, binding the generations.

When we finished, I exited the booth and we relocated back to Frazier's main desk, where he manually transcribed the results of my examination onto a form summarizing outcomes and recommendations. The first and largest graph was an audiogram showing my hearing threshold at different sound frequencies, with the vertical axis labeled Hearing Level in Decibels and the horizontal, Pure Tone Audiometry. He used two different pens to draw two nearly overlapping dotted lines, one with red O's (my right ear) and one with blue X's (my left ear). Although the two lines meandered slightly up and down, like footprints left by tiny plovers on the beach, both fell entirely within the shaded gray zone at the top, indicating the lowest decibel range, from −10 to 20.

Zero decibels, I discover, does not equal *no* sound; rather, it's the threshold of hearing, of perceptible sound, for the healthy adult ear. And if you can hear sounds below that, *mazel tov!*—your hearing is better than average.

"So," Frazier concluded with a smile, spinning the page in my direction so that I could read it, "your hearing is normal. Anything within this area is normal."

Although I won't be needing further attention for my hearing, those who do need such attention will be fortunate to get it from Dr. Frazier.

Haunt

Traverse City, MI

BRIAN CZYZYK

The belly of my old school is empty:
peach tiles fissured sixty different ways,
no books in the library, no stink of wax
in the gym. I open my mouth to the spout
of a drinking fountain, but nothing comes.

Back then, I didn't care that the water was poisoned.
I never guessed the bleach from the laundromat
next door would seep into the wells buried
under the monkey bars and soccer field.

I remember tangles of wild grapes
draped over the chain link edge
of the playground. How I crushed
palmfuls of berries when no one would speak
to me: the boy picked last for basketball,
the boy who wheezed five minutes in
to the pacer test, the boy who never dared
to raise his hand and name Madrid as Spain's capital.

Back then, water was medicine. The only thing
to ease the heave of lungs, the itch in my throat.
Thirst is the body's cry to hold something
untamable. Maybe I'm still trying to wash
myself of all the words that never came.

Library Page

Akron, OH

L.S. QUINN

I am fifteen years old. It's October 1994. I'm wearing a flowered blue broomstick skirt, a nubbly woven tunic, and a black ribbon choker. Also, rebelliously, Birkenstock sandals and wool socks. My classmates and I have been fighting the administration for weeks over the new ban on open-toed shoes.

It's snowing, and the school has been waiting us out, assuming we would eventually see sense: fashion's not worth frostbite. But it's warm; the snow melts to grey-brown slush and mud on the sidewalks and tree lawns, and we don't care. We call a tree lawn a devil strip, here, just south of Akron. We call our school Hoover, after the Hoover company—our parents still make vacuum cleaners. Maytag hasn't yet scooped up that prize and moved our jobs to Juarez. I have never heard of a payday loan—we cash our checks at the savings and loan in the town square, next to the public library, the YMCA and St. Paul's Catholic Church.

I'm a page in the dim school library. There are no windows, and the lights are fluorescent, glowing green and purple. I check books in; I check books out. We still use stamps and cards. Sometimes I spend study hall chiseling date stickers off the hardbacks, but mostly I hand out *Seventeen* and *YM*. I asked the librarian to order *Sassy*, but there was a blowjob joke in Issue 10, so she said no. She is stern and gray-haired, with an unfortunate bob, but she has a daughter. She must be human. She did understand the word "beej." It wasn't in the dictionary, a huge oyster-colored book on a stand near the copier.

The copier is miraculous—you can actually make a legible copy from a book, because the hinge of the lid extends to fit even the dictionary. You do have to mash the spine down to get two pages at once. This is severely frowned upon. So when I make copies, I tediously open the book and flip it over. Copy, flip. Copy, flip. Clunk it shut. I am allowed to make copies for other students, for ten cents apiece. They stand and wait, and the less-desirable boys flirt with me. I never understand why the dullest and stupidest boys want to ask me out. It's baffling. It doesn't occur to me they are not exclusively interested in conversation. I know I am a strange girl, and cripplingly intelligent—I have placed fourteenth in the national spelling bee—but I have no idea that I'm also beautiful, and that the combination is attractive to men and women alike.

I myself have crushes on men and women alike—I am a sucker for skater boys' bowl cuts and for the pixie on our school's only lesbian. Our school's only lesbian sits on the radiator in Classical Literature and argues philosophy and religion with me. She doesn't seem to notice I'm flirting. I desperately hope no one else notices either. But on Thursday nights when her swim meets are coming up, I angrily contemplate baking her a shoe-box of cookies, to wrap in foil and decorate with orange and black ribbon. This is how girls demonstrate affection, by baking cookies for their football-playing boyfriends. I have never had a football-playing boyfriend. A halfback asked me out once, but I didn't realize he was serious, so I said no. I never bake those cookies.

I do bake a cake for our Charles Dickens unit, and decorate it for Miss Havisham's wedding. In that English class, taught by another stern woman, I don't bother to take notes. I'm shocked when we're told to turn them in at the end of the semester. I panic, and I ask if I can copy Christopher's. Our teacher grudgingly agrees. Chris loans me his notebook during lunch, and I copy and flip. Copy and flip. In sixth period the teacher's mouth drops open: she had not expected a sheaf of Xeroxes. It had not occurred to me to do it by hand. What would be the point?

What *is* the point? I develop a deep depression, and debate suicide. I go to my morning job, the breakfast shift at McDonald's, and try to slit my wrists in the break room. The knife is dull, though, and it hurts too much. I go to K-mart and try to buy a hunting knife, but I don't have enough money. Instead I go to school and pull my best friend out of class. Marnie tells me that I will never be alone; that I am not the only person in the world who feels this way. This is comforting, rather than frightening. She also tells me that Death is my friend and will never leave me, will always be there. That suicide will always be an option, so there's no need to take it right now. This is also comforting, rather than frightening—I can put off killing myself, because I can always do it tomorrow, or next week, or next year. This saves my life.

My life goes on, often in libraries—I learn to make files for the reference department. We own a machine that reads the new CD-ROMs, so we have an electronic encyclopedia, but for current events, we read the newspaper. The librarian marks certain articles in red pen, and we cut them out with an X-acto knife. She glues them to pieces of cardstock, color-coded by subject, and we file them in deep drawers by the dictionary. We have two copies of each newspaper—the *New York Times*, the *Washington Post*, the *Wall Street Journal*. This way we can get both sides of an article, follow the jump—we slice and flip. Slice and flip. Then glue, and flip again.

Decades later, in the big-city library, where I am being paid to check books in and check books out, the branch clerk is going through the newspaper. I hear the page flip and for a moment she is cutting it with an X-acto knife, ready to glue it to cardstock and put it in a file. But then my barcode scanner beeps and a receipt whirrs out of the printer. Yendas Harper, an old man, unshaven and unwashed, has checked out eight Blu-Rays, all horror. I know he is about to ask me out, and I will decline, referring to a boyfriend I don't have any more. I don't have a girlfriend, either, but I do have an ex-wife.

I have an ex-wife and a Tinder account, a college degree and a car. I wear pinup dresses and cashmere cardigans; I know now why men ask me out. I wear lip stain and put my hair in a flip, copying videos online. I help strangers send faxes, help them do their taxes, feed children free lunches—a sandwich, an apple, and a pint of milk. We have an Xbox and a giant flat-screen TV and an origami class. There's a payday loan store on the corner, across from the school, the abortion clinic and the New Hope House of Prayer Holiness Temple of God: All Are Welcome. I leaf through brochures from health fairs and GED classes, squaring them off and stacking them high. My life goes on in the library—Death may be a friend, but he's one I've lost touch with over the years. I had lost touch with the football player and the school lesbian, I'd lost touch with the teachers and even my best friend, but now there's Facebook and Twitter and Instagram, and we constantly gossip, tell jokes and share pictures of food. We talk about the best way to fight this dystopian administration. We are determined not to just wait it out. Today the snow is melting off the sidewalks and devil strips and I'm wearing open-toed shoes. Tomorrow will be sunny and we'll open the clerestory windows, let the light come streaming in over the shelves. Tomorrow I'll judge a spelling bee and teach a man to use a mouse. I'll pause for a moment and listen to the branch clerk, as she opens the newspaper, beginning to read and flip. Read and flip. Read and flip. Read and flip.

"Other" Confusion

Toledo, OH

KAY PATTERSON

It was an evening like so many others in my sixteenth year: meatloaf for supper in the kitchen of our split-level home at the edge of the city, then upstairs to my bedroom for homework. There was a soft knock on the door and my usually assertive mother came in on little cat's feet bearing a booklet.

"Dr. Fries gave me this," she said, her tone hushed and timid. "Read it, then give it to your brother." She didn't hand it to me, she set it down on the corner of my desk.

Talking to Your Teenager about Sex. Before I could unglue my eyes from the cover, Mom had crept back out, closing the door with a quiet, but definitive snap.

Try as I might, I couldn't return to that math problem with *Talking to Your Teenager about Sex* staring at me. I flipped it open and pored over the Table of Contents looking for the chapter "How to Do It." No luck. I was going to have to read it page by page.

During that exercise, I ran across a chapter—is it a chapter if it's half a page long?—called "Other." Under a graphic of two men peering longingly at each other: "There are a few people in the world, very few, who are attracted to people of their own sex."

Huh? I was having enough trouble figuring out the male/female thing. It was 1963 and my parents, like the Beav's, slept in twin beds. TV? The raciest thing was the Beav's parents, talking in their bedroom. They were fully clothed and standing. I had had no dates, so I had no training wheels on my hormones.

At Roy C. Start High School, where I rushed through the halls with 2,000 other kids, the only romance I saw was boys with girls and vice versa.

I decided to ignore "Other." It made no sense at all.

I was horrified that Mom wanted me to give this book to my 17-year-old brother. Did I gather my nerve, walk across the hall and quietly place it on the corner of his desk? Memory fails me.

Queer at the County Fair

Licking County, Ohio

NICHOLE LOHRMAN-NOVAK AND JANINE TIFFE

Since the establishment of the Licking County 4-H Band in 1948, it has grown into a staple of its community in rural central Ohio. Located east of Columbus, the band is open to adolescents between the ages of 11-19. Beginning in the 1980s, it has gradually yet increasingly become a queer safe space for local youth. Many attribute this phenomenon, in part, to band director Jane Copenhefer, who has led the group since 1986, and her wife, Dannette Morehouse, who became a band advisor in 1999.

Ethnomusicology professor Janine Tiffe (Kent State University) and music education professor David Knapp (Syracuse University) interviewed members of the 4-H Band during the agriculturally-centric Hartford Fair in 2017. Excerpts of those interviews are embedded within Nichole Lohrman-Novak's recollections of her own time in the band.

September 2004

I'm sitting in the computer lab of my college dorm when my Samsung flip phone starts to ring. It's not late for me, but it seems late for people not on a college schedule. I'm delighted to see David Shane's name scroll across the circular screen. I flip open my phone and begin my usual David Shane-greeting with just the right variation in pitch and tone to show my enthusiasm to talk to him. Before I can get the "ane..." of David Shane out, I'm interrupted.

"It's Becky."

"Oh! Hi Becky! What are you guys doing?" I say, noticing the juxtaposition of her serious tone and the voices in the background on her end of the phone.

"We're with Jane and Dannette at The Colonizer. He just told them about moving to New York —"

"Does that mean he's decided for sure?"

"I don't really think so, but listen. David's really drunk, and he wants to tell Jane and Dannette about you..."

"About me? Ummm, I don't —"

"That's why I'm calling you. I told David he can't tell them for you. It's your news to tell," she asserted.

"Well, but maybe it would be nicer to have someone else tell them for me, like they would just already know when I see them again," I respond as a half-question.

"It's whatever you want to do, but I'm not letting David tell them unless you want him to." Her level of authority is tangible—even over the phone.

I think for a minute. *Will they be upset with me?*

(On Jane as Mentor)
Jane is one of my favorite people in the world.
She's a mother figure like no other. I have the
deepest respect for Jane and everything that she
does. She's changed so many lives. She is one of the
kindest people I've ever met. I can't say
enough good things about her.

—Band Member

They know too many other gay people to be mad at me for being gay. *Will they be mad that I didn't tell them sooner? Is it wrong that I want David to tell them for me?* It seems like they're having a good time, and I'm sure David will have a much more entertaining way of telling them than I would...

I bring my attention back to the phone. Everyone is laughing now. While trying to compose herself from the laughter, Becky tells me that David has just poured sugar instead of salt onto his fries. I can't help but laugh. I think about how odd it is that I'm sitting in the quiet lobby of my dorm in Bowling Green, but I'm imagining myself sitting at "our table" at The Colonizer in Newark.

I hear David in the background pleading. I ask Becky to let me talk to him.

"Nichoooooole," David drunkenly sings, beautifully. "Can I please tell them?"

"You promise not to tell too much?"

"Of course!" *When did he start sounding so grown-up?*

"Okay. You can tell them, but promise to leave out all the ridiculousness."

"Ahhhhh—I love you, I love you, I love you!" he exclaims.

"And don't let them think I didn't tell them because I was worried about —"

"It's me," Becky interrupts. "I'll make sure they know you weren't not telling them."

"Thanks, Becky. Let me know what they say." Worry begins to set in.

"I will. They'll be fine. It's not like they don't know everyone in 4-H Band is gay," she offers our running joke as a calming assurance.

(On 4-H Band Queerness)
If we list[ed] all former [4-H Band] presidents,
[and then removed those] who had been gay,
I would imagine it'd be down to a quarter [of the names].

Is that because gay people are better leaders?
Or is that how many gays are here?

Well, this is just a tiny little farm community.
There is one county-wide artistic outlet that
still is under the bridge of 4-H. It's the biggest
artistic outlet in a tiny, little, anti-gay
community.
—Dialog Between Band Alumnus & Interviewer

August 2002 - (Fair Week)

It's quiet time in the dorms. Normally, I would be sleeping; I don't know what's wrong with me. Maybe it's that we're midway through the fair, maybe it's the heat, for sure, the air from everyone's oscillating fans isn't helping me. I don't know though; today I just can't seem to quit thinking...about Ashley.

The weird thing about this crush, or whatever it is, is that I know people in the band would support me. There are so many gay boys in band. I could talk to David or Trashy or Mark or maybe Bart—anyone, really...

(On Traditional Masculinity)
Interviewer: I've only been here a few days and I
don't really know this area that well, but I'm seeing
dudes cuddling in bed - straight dudes. They're
totally bro-ing out. They were halfway naked and
then just hanging out, and the guy over here is, I'm
thinking he's known to be gay...so they're being
half-naked and physical with this other half-naked
guy who's gay, and there's no problems.

—Interviewer

...and I think Jane and Dannette would be, too. The problem is I don't think I should talk to gay people—or people with gay friends. I know it's okay to be gay, but how do I know if I'll go to Hell for it? I need someone who gets where I'm coming from as a Christian. If I weren't in love with Ashley, she'd be the perfect person to talk to about this.

(On Tolerance)
It seems as though you were saying that you've
learned about tolerance by being in this band.

Yes, I would definitely say that. OK, I'm raised in a
Christian background and I wouldn't generally...A
lot of the views and the band don't agree with what
I agree with, [but] it does seem like when people
are arguing in public, people are dehumanized,
and nobody ever thinks about the fact that they're
talking about a person, not a thing. I think that's
what's impacted me the greatest. It's not, they're
not ideas anymore. You start seeing everybody else's
opinions and it's not just an opinion anymore, it's a
person with an opinion.

—Dialog Between Band Member & Interviewer

I stare up at the ceiling, and tears start to roll from the corners of my eyes. I need to stop this. I sit up to grab a tissue from my footlocker, and notice Amy, writing in a notebook, on her bed. That's it! *Amy* is who I need to talk to! She's clearly a better Christian than I am, and even though Trashy broke her heart when he came out, she's still nice to all the gay boys in band, including Trashy. Before I overthink it, I lean over toward her bed and ask if we can talk.

"Yeah, what's going on?" she whispers. It's quiet time, we have to stay quiet-ish.

"I kind of wanted to ask your opinion about something. It's really out of nowhere, so if you're not comfortable, or don't want to, I totally understand," I say, fumbling over my words as I contemplate what a bad idea this is.

"Umm, okay," she responds with an awkward giggle of confusion.

"Okay..." *What am I doing?!* "Well, I kind of think I might be...gay."

SILENCE. Her face looks surprised, but not painfully so—and not angry at all. I start to feel a tinge of relief.

"And, I'm...worried," I sound like I'm asking, "about going to Hell..." As the words leave my mouth, I start to wonder which revelation sounds more ridiculous, being gay or being worried about Hell.

More silence, but this feels more contemplative than surprised. I notice the pressure to fill the space with more of my own thoughts, but I decide against it. I work hard not to cry while waiting for her to tell me what she's thinking.

"Well..." she starts, "I can understand why you might be worried, but what makes you think you're gay?"

"Ashley," I whisper.

"Oh. That makes sense. Are you guys like together?"

Her question lands painfully. I can't even tell Ashley how I feel, let alone *be* together. I think about how odd it is that so many people at school think Ashley and I are together, even though I'm terrified to be a lesbian.

"No," I finally say. "I haven't told her how I feel. That's kind of why I wanted to talk to you. I really want to tell her, but I'm terrified that she will end our friendship completely...

(On Friendship)
This band really does create good friendships and
memories. This group...you don't come in here and
not talk to anybody, because they're gonna get you
to come out of your shell, and they're going to get
you to talk.

—Band Alumnus

...and what if I'm not gay? What if I'm just confused, and I do all this and just end up looking stupid?"

I realize I've been staring at the cement floor, and finally look up to make eye contact with Amy. She looks genuinely concerned. I start to feel really relieved and comfortable to have her helping me now. And then I remember how shitty she must feel because of everything that happened with Trashy, and immediately feel guilty.

"I'm really sorry," I interrupt. "This has to be really hard for you. I shouldn't have asked you about all this."

"No, you're fine. I still wish it could have ended better, but it's okay."

I'm so impressed by Amy's maturity—like all the time—but being able to be "okay" around Trashy is extra impressive.

Amy asks me what makes me think I'm in love with Ashley. I start thinking about all the reasons, but feel like they would sound stupid if I say them out loud. I tell Amy it's hard to explain, but I feel like I need Ashely in a deeper way than just a friend. I start to tell her about my sad ritual of listening to Sarah McLachlan and crying myself to sleep thinking of Ashley. I tell her about how the night before last, I was talking to Ashley outside of the regular 4-H dorms, and I really almost told her. The demolition derby was going on at the grandstand; we could hear it in the background, but it wasn't so loud we couldn't hear each other. She told me how she had done in her dairy feeder show and how she was going to show again the next day. The way the flood lights from the dorm landed on her, she looked... perfect. It felt like the right time to tell her. But I didn't. I was too afraid of ruining everything. There is really no reason for me to put my problems on Ashley like that.

I realize that I have left the conversation with Amy. In talking about Ashley, I was in *that* moment with *her*, instead of *this* moment with Amy. I look up at her and notice she looks deep in thought.

August 2007

The drive from Bowling Green to Croton is filled with farmland, sprinkled with small towns and rest stops. I'm reminded of the time I snuck back down for the last concert the same weekend I moved into college, my freshman year. My mom was adamant that I needed to stay in Bowling Green to get acclimated. She was also pretty adamant that I not get my nose pierced—that was a tough weekend for my mom's wishes.

On this day, the drive is much more exciting. Dan and Megan are with me. I feel simultaneously excited and incredibly self-conscious to show them this oddly rural part of my life. Dan was in his high school band, but it's really hard to explain 4-H band to college friends, even if they played in a band themselves. Megan, well...I'm excited to share everything with Megan. We've been dating for 2 months now. This summer, with her, has been the most glorious time of my life.

Megan has already met Jane and Dannette. She was in my room with me the night Jane called to *finally* come out to me. Jane knew I already knew—Dannette told me a couple of years ago that they were, and had been, together (the "roommates" story really was a lie!), but it was still nice that Jane cared enough to tell me herself. Of course, Megan was thoroughly confused about why it was such a big deal that these two were lesbians. I told her it was hard to explain...and then went on to explain it.

This will be Megan's second time at the Hartford fairgrounds. We were just here a few weeks ago. That's when she met Jane and Dannette, actually. We stayed at their house, and then helped them bring mulch out to the fairgrounds to get ready for a work party. For a city girl, Megan looks comfortable spreading mulch at the county fair. That was also the first real time I'd been around Jane and Dannette as a couple. Clearly, they've been a couple for years, but there's something about seeing them more relaxed and affectionate that both surprised and relieved me.

As soon as we pull into the fairgrounds, Dannette spots us and walks over to the car. We hug, and she fills me in on whatever minor drama has arisen. Carrying my trombone has always made me self-conscious, but the way Megan watches me with it is too sweet for me to worry too much. I make some sarcastic "welcome to my childhood" comment, and the three of us walk up toward Tara, the 4-H Band's amphitheater.

In the years since my time in the band, Megan and I (now married) have remained close friends with Jane and Dannette, and continue to help out with the band when we can. And, of course, Megan still thinks it's cute when I play trombone at alumni events.

Over the years, Jane and Dannette have become more open in their identity as a couple, and although they have never done anything in particular for the LGBTQ-A youth in the band, the welcoming atmosphere they've created is especially significant for those members.

In 2009, Jane proposed to Dannette, and while they were still fairly closeted in public, they began to relax more within select circles, usually comprised of queer 4-H Band alumni.

In 2015, months after the *Obergefell v Hodges* Supreme Court decision made same-sex marriage legal across the country, Jane and Dannette were married at Camp Ohio, a beautiful 4-H campgounds in St. Louisville—and the location of 4-H band camp for decades. Many alumni and current band members attended, and even performed together as musicians for the ceremony. Megan and I were their "best women."

Jane and Dannette no longer try to hide their relationship. They love each other openly, demonstrating the importance of accepting and being secure with oneself; one can be queer and still be a valuable member of a larger rural community.

In 2019, as I do most years, I went to band camp to help. This year, though, this year felt different. I heard kids telling one another "Happy Pride." I saw more queer kids being visible within their friend groups, and then right before an afternoon practice, I watched as two kids ran up to Tara. Both kids were wearing flags as capes: one, the rainbow pride flag; the other, the trans pride flag.

And it hit me.

How far we've all come, that in the same county, in the same 4-H club, with the same director, that *these kids* feel so comfortable and accepted and loved just 15 years after my own struggle...it's astonishing. Yes, there have been important legal cases, legislation, cultural shifts in the last 15 years, but the constant is that young musicians of Licking County, Ohio know, and have always known, we can be ourselves here.

Tommie and Jane

Cape Girardeau, MO

SHARON SEITHEL

"Tommie" started walking around my neighborhood when I was about twelve. I remember that she was always dressed in a tan trench coat, slacks and sensible shoes. Her walk seemed to be one with purpose, head down. She did not meet my gaze when we met on the sidewalk. I had heard she had a heart attack and suspected that the walking was a suggestion from the doctor. Tommie and Jane were my next door neighbors for eighteen years. In researching their lives, I found that the two women bought the house on Sunset Blvd. in Cape Girardeau, Missouri during the thirties. My parents bought the house next door in the late fifties and I was born a few years later. I didn't know it then, but Tommie's given name was Elaine Davis, and Jane was Mary Jane Barnett. But to me, they were just my neighbors, Tommie and Jane.

I was a full on "tomboy" preferring to play cowboy or soldier and wear pants when I could get away with it. I had a Gene Autry revolver, a rifle, a football and my Dad's WWII military gear. He indulged and my mother tolerated most of my childhood loves. There was never once a word about my boyish ways that connected me to Tommie, who was clearly the butch in relationship.

I was fascinated. I never had much interaction with her—noticing that she was much more masculine in appearance, I'd wonder if things would have been different if I were a boy. Jane, on the other hand, was friendly and always bought a box or two of Girl Scout cookies when I knocked on their door each year. I knew Jane was different because she was fabulously feminine. My mother wore practical scarves and skirts. But Jane was glamorous, and more than once I saw her leave the house in what I can only assume was a mink fur coat. They drove a white Lincoln Town car, which was not a common vehicle found in our working class neighborhood. They were quiet neighbors and now knowing they were born just after the turn of the century, I realize they were in their fifties and sixties when I was a kid.

Cape was an idyllic place to grow up. It is a college town on the Mississippi River that is just small enough that everyone knows of everyone, but just big enough for a little bit of anonymity. Every town has a Broadway, and Cape's version was that central corridor that ends at Main Street with a view of that big muddy river. The town was built around the river, the schools, and the church.

My understanding of Tommie and Jane was that they were moderately well off and the idea of anyone harassing them would have been beyond the pale for this small religious town. As much as I was aware that they were different, I didn't know—and couldn't imagine—if there were others like them in town. Friends didn't come over often, though I remember a handful of visitors in eighteen years.

Their house was just a little bigger and nicer than our house, white with red trim. In front was a huge evergreen that provided privacy and hid the entrance, like Tommie's downward gaze hid her eyes. My job each summer was to pull the weeds that grew on the fence line between our two properties. It usually took me a couple of days in the blazing summer sun but it gave me access to their backyard and I was always trying to catch a glimpse of either of them, but especially the elusive Tommie.

The spring and summer of 1978 was the beginning of my awakening. Until then, I don't have a memory of consciously connecting who I was to who Tommie and Jane were. I do have one very vivid memory around that time, the arrival of my date for the high school prom. I was going with a guy named Mark, not because being with him was important to me but I knew that being part of a prom was important to me. It was a rite of passage and I wanted to attend even if I knew that Mark wasn't my ideal date and a dress wasn't my ideal clothing.

My mom was overjoyed to help me buy a bright yellow prom dress. Mark came to pick me up and brought the standard prom corsage. Before we left, there were photos to take and we were outside in front of my house. I expected that I would be focused on the flowers, the dress, maybe even Mark. Instead, I was acutely aware of what Tommie and Jane might be thinking. On the surface I wanted them to see that I was not like them. Deep down, I think that might have been the moment that I realized that I was exactly like them and part of me wanted them to know it right then and there. I, too, would be the "town queer." When I fully came out a couple years later, we had moved to another part of Cape Girardeau. I never saw Tommie or Jane again.

Once I grew up, came out, settled down and found an outlet for my love of history, I became passionate about LGBTQ history. As I have had the privilege to capture the oral history of many lesbians who came of age in the sixties or earlier, I hear a common theme. They pretty consistently say that they were adults before they even realized there was such a thing as a same sex relationship. They knew they were different but didn't know how and the concept of women living together as partners was a virtual unknown. But for me, that was not the case. I always knew there was such a thing. For better or worse, I had the "queers next door," as my dad fondly—truly, fondly— called them. I say fondly because it was never said in malice or to denigrate them. He simply didn't have another word. He could have lied and suggested to me that they were sisters but he didn't. For that I am grateful.

Over the years, I often thought of dropping in on Jane as I had heard that Tommie passed away. But I never did, and she passed in 1997. It is one of my great regrets. I am deeply sorry to have missed talking to Jane and hearing her fascinating life story. She was truly an out lesbian that was born in 1908 in the Missouri Bootheel. She then spent most of her adult years in my conservative small town of Cape Girardeau. As far as I have found, Tommie seems to have been originally from Cape Girardeau. They were both great supporters of the arts and owned a downtown store called the Co-op. My history friends helped with some research, and we did find articles about social visits that Jane made in her youth, which mentioned Tommie. The Missouri Historical Society holds a collection of Mary Jane Barnett's photos and each one leaves me in awe: women picnicking together, some wearing masculine clothes. One amazing photo is a group of women at the Colony Club in 1938. Jane and Tommie are in that photo, and it was my favorite. Research points to it being the kind of place in East Cape Girardeau, Illinois that might have catered to gay clientele. It was a posh nightclub, and there seemed to be gambling and other typical vices of East Cape. The place burned down in 1958.

State Historical Society of Missouri - Cape Girardeau

Cape Girardeau, like most small towns, has passed on a mixed legacy. Tommie and Jane found a safe place to live and prosper. I was able to see what might be possible and I think living next door to them shaped my view of the world in ways that I am still coming to terms with. During this time, someone who would become very famous was also growing up just a few blocks away and only a few years older than me. Rush Limbaugh is also a product of Cape Girardeau and I suspect that his childhood experience mirrored some of the same cultural and religious mores that impacted me. I often think of how different our worldviews turned out to be; Rush and I. I also sometimes think about how lucky I was to live next door to Tommie and Jane. It is possible that without a view into their lives and what I always believed to be their love, I might have accepted a narrative that told a very different story about what was possible in life—in my life. I wonder if anything would have turned out differently if it had been Rush, and not me, who had them as neighbors?

Jane and Tommie, 1930s

Tommie and Jane, 1938

Jane and Tommie outside their house on Sunset Blvd., 1950

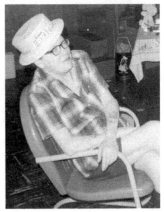

Tommie and Jane, 1960s

Jane and Tommie, 1960s

Jane, 1990

Persimmon

Scaly Mountain, NC

JEFFERY BEAM

For about fifty feet above me the straight trunk rises with its scaly square bark. This edge of the field has already turned brown. The first frost and a short autumn rain last week made sure of that. All color has taken to air, splattering the nearby woods with yellow, gold, and ruddy red. Some people call this tree "possumwood" because our nocturnal friend so fondly sleeps in its branches. It's commonly called "persimmon," an old Algonquian name. Its leaves fell earlier.

The limbs splay out, mad and snaky. The sun sinks behind it, and from my footing in the field, it seems a thousand Chinese lanterns light up. "Fruit of the Gods" the Algonquian called it. Only the virtuous could eat such clean, orange fruit—a defenseless layer of earth's cool breath dusting its flesh. Only a possum dare sleep in such branches.

The loveless have friends in fields with persimmons at the edges, where all loss gathers in burly branches shot through with a natural sorrow. My friend, nothing so bleak as bare trees will do for you; but this one, whose laden fruit, warmly colored, sour before frost, wrought with poison, is sweet to the mouth now. The year in ruin. A field never before known. Trembling in silence.

Jeffery Beam ©2010, *The Broken Flower*, Skysill Press (England)

In This Dream House

North Dakota

MICHAEL SCHREIBER

What ghosts linger here in this Dream House?

It's a natural question to ask in a hundred-year-old house, especially in this bedroom in which two lovers have now died. One of them, my beloved friend Bernard, recently passed peacefully at 95 in his bed under a portrait of the other, his adored Bud, who died less peacefully at age 36 in this room some thirty years ago. I did not know Bud, and yet I do; and not only from the stories Bernard told me about the life and love they shared here in what Bernard called his "Dream House."

I grew up in a house even older than this in North Dakota, one that creaked and moaned its indecipherable secrets throughout the night as I lay wide-eyed in my bed wondering who (or what) might be lurking behind the closet door, or in the attic, or even under the bed itself. It was an otherwise happy home, made so by my family and the richness of my childhood imagination and play in its every room. But there was always something forlorn about its dark corners; always a sense of being observed somehow. On one of my sleepless childhood nights, I'd actually (or think I may have) seen someone, some *thing*, in the hall outside my open bedroom door, pausing to look in at me. A woman, yet not quite a physical being. It may have been a dream, of course, but it was still a well-remembered image in my mind when, a few years later, my father found a cache of old letters hidden under the floorboards of our attic.

The letters had evidently been secreted away up there by their recipient, a young woman named Anna, who was likely a boarder in the house during its previous incarnation as a rooming house during the First World War. The letters told the tale of an ill-fated love affair: her lover was not only married, but fearful of being drafted, and together he and she were plotting their escape from the war and his wife to Canada. Despite some sleuthing into old residential records and newspapers in my town's library, I was never able to find out their identities, or what became of their plan. Perhaps he had been sent off to war after all and had never returned, or perhaps he had fallen in the great pandemic of their time, the Spanish influenza. And perhaps she too had then passed on in her home, although hadn't really left. Was she my watcher in the corner, my visitor in the night?

Or perhaps she wasn't my ghost at all, but instead was the proprietress of the rooming house: a woman whose teenage son, I discovered in looking through those old newspapers, had died of a "sudden illness" and was laid out "for callers to view in the parlor"—my childhood living room. Under other floorboards in the attic, my father had also discovered a small crystal bowl filled with a boy's treasures: marbles; a stick of gum; a dog tag from 1912; a lighter; gumballs. "Adventure" magazines of the era were also found hidden behind a false wall in the closet of my bedroom; likely his room too. Was I being watched over by another mother? Perhaps so. But oddly, once the house revealed these secrets, it quieted. The sense of something apart from me and my family there departed once these artifacts were uncovered and I chose to cherish them. Who knows—perhaps my doing so unintentionally gave whomever was lingering there her release at long last. The passing of a torch, in a way: the stewardship of her own dream, now handed off to me.

Now I am to be the caretaker of yet another dream, as I pack up Bud's things along with Bernard's, to hopefully leave *this* Dream House at peace for its next owners. I have found Bud's leavings scattered everywhere amongst Bernard's: his wallet, ID, keys, jewelry, clothes, photos, papers. I even found an actual piece of Bud himself: a lock of his brown-blond hair, sealed in a yellowed envelope that Bernard dated just a month prior to Bud's death. A bundle of his letters to Bernard was also discovered in the attic—the eerie irony of this is certainly not lost on me— as were other mementos from Bud's very full if much too brief life. But more haunting is the paperwork I have found that accompanied Bud's long process of dying: insurance forms; medication schedules; routers of the devoted hospice nurses who aided Bernard's courageous effort to care for Bud through the end in his own home. Bernard was the first person in his state to privately care for an AIDS patient. The final items in this inventory are a photograph of Bud's name painted on the early AIDS quilt, and a postcard view of the whole enormous quilt stretched out to cover the National Mall in Washington, D.C. Bud's grave-sized panel on the quilt is but one of indiscernible thousands in the vast patchwork below.

But as this house too is yielding its secrets, I already detect nothing but great peace here. It's palpable as one moves from room to room in this Dream House: there's no feeling of anything watching or lingering or moving through. This has always been a well-loved space, a retreat and a playground, and that sense about it remains, in spite of Bud's turbulent, painful departure from it, and the debilitating grief that overtook Bernard here in the immediate years that followed. Ultimately, time eased Bernard's suffering over Bud, and his embracing of his own survival and his memories of their love brought life and light back into the house. Unlike my childhood home, love, not loss, seems to have won the day in this house. The night, too: I've always slept well here, even now when I've been alone in the house, curled up in Bernard and Bud's bed, with boxes of their cherished effects piled high all around me. There are no bumps in the night; no monsters under the bed or in the closet; only space for dreams.

A Dream House, indeed.

Bernie, IN

JAMES SCHWARTZ

The Schwartz Family history book,
Describes our settler forbearers thus:

"*The* ▬▬▬ *were only forty years removed*
When the Schwartz's settled Berne, Indiana"

Old Order colonization for an alpine messiah,
Worth crossing an ocean for,

Worth dying for, worth crying for,
On sacred ground not their own...

Letter to the Prodigal Son

Amish Country

ANONYMOUS

I saw you standing there, all alone at the edge of the crowd. Your somber look and downcast eyes matched the slump of your shoulders. You looked defeated. It was at one of the weddings in our neighborhood earlier last year—one of those perfect early summer days before it gets so warm and humid; the scent of newly mown hay mingling with the aroma of chicken frying for the meal; the hum of conversation and laughter, and the grinding of buggy wheels over gravel as the last of the invited guests arrived. You have no idea how I wanted to walk across the barnyard and stand beside you to give you a smile and tell you you're not alone, but never before did I feel our peoples' invisible barriers of age and marital status as much as I did that evening. I didn't dare draw any attention to myself, and would not have wanted to put any more pressure on you. I tried to catch your eye, hoping I could at least give you a smile, but your eyes never left the ground. But I want you to know that I think you are brave.

When I heard you had left, there wasn't much said. You were just one of those boys who craved a life outside of our community. I assumed you'd gone for the "usual": the English clothes, the car, the music, the TV, and a life without being told what to do and how to do it. You were just one of the many who leave and perhaps you'd be one of the ones who eventually returns. I sympathize with the ones who leave but I understand why those who return do as well. Our life is not the easiest, maybe, but it's hard to walk away from everything and everyone you've ever known. I get it.

In time, the grapevine rustled with rumors. There was maybe more to it, some said. Then came the hushed whispers. "He lives with another man." Then there were the knowing looks, the sighs and head-shakes. "He's a *gay*," they whispered. And inside I cried for you. I cried for me. I know how easily I could lose it all, too, because I, too, am gay. Being found out would mean excommunication and the loss of my job, family, and friends; being "put out of the church" and "given over to the Devil and all his angels."

You know how our people are. They can gossip, but when something like this happens among us, no one knows what to say, for "such things" aren't *supposed* to be found among us. These are situations one expects the English to deal with, but not good Amish families. So many of our people don't know how to react when the "sins" they associate with "the world" appear in our own communities. But we are here. I have a few precious memories tucked away, of conversation with others who accepted me for who I am—all of me—along with a few memories from my own youth of awkward, hurried encounters in dark and quiet places in my own community.

If only I had known what you were carrying all alone. I know what it's like: the guilt, shame, fear, and despair. If only I could have had a few words with you, a chance to tell you that this is not your fault or anything that you can change. I would have wanted to put a hand on your shoulder and look you in the eye and tell you, "You are a good person. You deserve to know that. This part of you we don't understand is as much a part of you as your brown eyes or your height. Don't be ashamed of who and what you are." I would want to tell you what I so badly needed to hear when I was your age. But I didn't know. Just like you don't know about me. You and I are alike in this way. We live in a big community and are surrounded by others, yet we are alone.

I understand your wanting to leave. While others whispered and others told your parents they were lifting them up in prayer, I was hoping you'd make it on the outside; that you'd find acceptance and support; that you'd find peace. I admired your courage.

And then you came back.

Life "out there" was harder than you expected, perhaps. It's a different world and you stepped out into it with very little awareness of how to make it. While others told your family how thankful they were to hear you'd returned and awkwardly asked how you were doing, I brushed away tears, for I hoped you could make it out there.

I hear things. I hear how your family takes you for counseling. I hear how they watch your comings and goings very closely. I hear how they plead with you to renounce your "sin" and join the church. But my pleadings are different. I would plead that you not give up, that you might use this time to make plans, that you might find the courage to leave again and that *this* time you'll make it. My pleading would be that you not be too hard on yourself and that you might accept yourself for who and what you are. Don't let them convince you that you should be ashamed of yourself or that you are lost and damned. My wish is to see you be able to be yourself among people who won't condemn you for what you cannot change. Part of me sees so much of my past in the struggles you are facing now. I see myself in you and I do not want you to be looking back with pangs of regret and sadness as I now do; regret for who and what I might be had I found the courage to leave and been granted the freedom to be myself. It may be too late for me, but within I have a strong desire to see you do what I failed to do.

I do not know why I was made this way. I do know that I didn't choose it. If renouncing my "sin" and fervent prayers could have taken this from me, it would have been lifted from my shoulders many years ago. I have finally come to accept who and what I am. The words to the German hymn I've heard countless times hit me hard the evening of that wedding: *Gott ist die Liebe, Er liebt auch mich!* (God is love, He loves me, too!) I looked across the crowd at you as they sang that evening and was deeply stirred. He loves *us*, too.

Please. Don't give up. Don't try to change who you are to make the Church or your parents happy. Please try again. And if you can make it out in the world, know that at least one man is inwardly cheering you on. Maybe you will be the success the others coming along behind need to look up to in order to find the courage to make their own escape. Until our people change, there is very little chance to find peace among us. We preach love and forgiveness, but we refuse to forgive the ones carrying their homosexuality alone. We can forgive any number of sins but this one and because our people won't forgive us, we must forgive ourselves.

And I ask you to forgive me. Perhaps if I had been more courageous, you might have had an example to look up to. But I failed. And I fail again in not telling you this face-to-face. But know that I am praying for you and I love you for who and what you are.

Humbly,

For Danni

Concord, NC

APRIL VAZQUEZ

When you were still a tiny seedling curled up inside me, the Mexican spiritualist held a silver chain over my swelling belly. *There's a strong masculine energy here*, she solemnly pronounced. *The baby will be a boy.*

But you weren't. At our next doctor visit, your father peered into the spectral ultrasound image, the pulsating heart at its center. *She'll play soccer, anyway,* he said stubbornly.

When you were a little sprout of four years, you were the prince in elaborate make-believe scenes acted out with your sister. That was the year you told us you'd never marry.

At six you made a collage of beautiful women cut from magazines. *Look at my sexy ladies,* you told me, lowering your voice on *sexy*. I put it in your baby box. It's there now, on top of the blue-and-pink-striped hospital toboggan and your first onesie, *Daddy's Little Princess* over the heart.

At eight you wanted to be Isaac Newton in the school play. *I look like him,* you protested when the teacher said no. *All the boys had long hair back then.* I agreed. We chalked it up to Mrs. Lambert's lack of imagination, but I knew what else might be there, lurking behind. Like the tea set an aunt bought for your birthday, the year you asked for a Spider-Man mask.

Late one afternoon when the sunlight was sparkling off the pond, you asked me, *What if I'm gay?*

Then... you are, I said, draping an arm over your shoulder.

We walked on, and after a while I added, *Uncle Paul is gay.*

I love Uncle Paul.

Me too.

And the one that does Dory's voice in the Nemo movie?

That's right. She's one of the coolest people I can think of.

You were satisfied.

You grew. New teeth replaced smaller, lost ones (carefully labeled by date in zip-loc bags in your baby box); you stretched upward, blossomed. Now you're a tall, willowy creature in whom I hardly recognize any sign of myself. A beauty, by anyone's standards.

Mom, can I talk to you? you ask one night. I look up from my book, blinking at being so suddenly drawn back to the here and now. You sit down on the bed beside me, push your bangs back absentmindedly. Your dark eyes are anxious, and I feel a flicker of fear myself. There's so much against you: the world's cruel prejudices, its judgment. It's hard enough to be a woman, any woman.

Then I rally. To hell with them. You have us on your side. Until my dying breath, you'll have me.

So I smile, take your hand. *Tell me about her,* I say.

For Dani first appeared in *Motherwell.*

Just Another Gay Story

Schiller Park, IL

SAMER HASSAN SALEH

You stand at your father's funeral, your best friend Gina beside you: a dark-skinned, long-haired, beautiful Latina. She towers over your family in 6 inch heels. Person after person walks down the line of grieving family members, shakes their hands, and gives their condolences. You are the last person in line but no one comes to you, you're ignored. Instead of sympathy, you receive piercing looks of hatred. Your aunt, the woman who used to change your diapers, whose son you used to play with as kids —your father's sister —stops mid-way into the hall and gives you a glare from across the room. You exchange eye-contact for what seems like eons. She mumbles something as she finally walks past you.

The family blames you for your father's death, whispers from the room reach your ears about how your father "couldn't handle the shame of having a gay son." "Shame, that's what it is? That's what killed my father?" you whisper to Gina, "It definitely wasn't the pack of cigarettes he smoked every day that had any impact on his health?"

You can't breathe, but you don't fight back. Not when your dad punches you in the face. Not when he wraps a belt around your neck and cuts your throat. Not when he drags you to the ground and knocks out your front teeth. Not when your mom joins in and steps on your genitals. You still don't fight back, even though you think you're going to die. Focus on the clock in the corner, focus on the ticking hands of the clock. You just couldn't see your parents as your enemies—as these cruel beings taking pleasure in your agony. Your dad would tighten the belt at any sign of movement, the sharp buckle cutting you ever deeper, blood trickling down your neck and staining your white shirt. You wore a white shirt today of all days, you never wear white. How do you get blood out of a white shirt? Tick tock. Your mind takes you away in order to save you and you focus on the clock in the corner, your eyes become glossy, fixed on the hands of the clock. "We know you're a whore," says your father. "We know all about your gay life," says

your mother. "America corrupted you," they scream into your ear. "We know you're having sex with hundreds of men! You're a prostitute!": unwarranted accusations that you agree with in order to get them to stop. You would agree to whatever absurdities they hurl at you, despite the fact that you're a virgin who only recently had your first kiss. You agree, just to get them to stop.

You would agree to anything just to get them to stop. Focus on the clock. The ordeal lasts two hours. Your parents had found out from your cousin that you are gay, and they threaten to kill you if you don't agree to go to shock therapy. You believe that you might die in a country where no one knows you, that your friends will never know what happened to you. You consent to the therapy out of fear for your life. It's 2009 and you're 18 years old— your baptism into adulthood is filled with blood. A few hours later, your father finally lets you out of the room so you can get your "faggot hair" cut off. As he takes you downstairs to make a phone call and go to the barber, you notice that he is distracted and that it might be your only chance to escape. You take it and bolt.

With blood running down your face, you zig-zag out of the hotel, your father's threat to shoot you if you ran away loud in your memory. For hours you wander the dilapidated streets of Barquisimeto, the city you were born in, constantly slowing from a sprint to a weak crawl, but when you think about whether your father is after you the sprint returns; you plead with people in broken Spanish for help. The indifference from the inhabitants of the barrio takes its toll until you squat on a street corner and cry.

All around you are bright colored, hacienda-style homes. Vibrant teals, yellows, greens, and burgundies converge to give the neighborhood a welcoming vibe. The road in front of you is a collage of hand carved stones, a puzzle with no symmetry. Each stone has its own unique personality. A clear blue sky hovers overhead, lush jungle blankets mountain ranges in the background— a true paradise. For you, it's hell on Earth.

The night before, you had attempted to return home to pay your respects, Gina at your side. Schiller Park, a neighborhood of cookie-cutter homes, oak-lined streets, and beautiful lawns cut by the same dads at the exact same time every week: a peaceful world. As you walked closer down the block, you realized that you weren't allowed. Inside your family home, your relatives had gathered and mourned together, the wailing of the women pierced the air as a community of support formed around your immediate family. They came to grieve and share in this difficult time. Cars were spilling out of the driveway and into the street, parked millimeters apart in order to make room for other mourners. The entire tribe had come from across the land to show their respect.

Your brother-in-law, who you hadn't seen in years, shouted from across the street: "Stay where you are, Samer! Do not come any closer." A step further would have warranted a call to the police, he said, this was private property. Your mother gave strict orders that you were not to be allowed inside. "I'm not even allowed in my own home," you said as your legs started trembling. You leaned against Gina and she propped you up as you walked away, shaking uncontrollably. You honored their wishes and grieved a distance away. Couldn't make a scene, mustn't shame the family.

Out of nowhere, guardian angels come upon you—a local family sweeps you up off the street corner, tends to your wounds, and drives you to an immigration lawyer who promises to help you get back to America. With your new-found lawyer's help, you convalesce for two weeks in military barracks and hotel rooms courtesy of the Venezuelan government.

He takes you to the American embassy to find answers, but the clerk says bluntly, "Buy a Spanish dictionary. Get a job." The ordeal of the last few weeks is too much— you snap. Your parents never got you a green card— it was just a lie to get you to leave the United States knowing full well that you were un-documented. You were never meant to return. You fling all the documents in your hands at the clerk's face. Security guards rush up to remove you from the building, threatening arrest.

Once they release you outside, you rush to the short fence surrounding the embassy, clamber over it, and threaten to jump off the cliffside in a desperate effort to be taken seriously. As a large crowd begins to form, finally a diplomat emerges from the embassy and gives you a hopeful answer to talk you back over the fence. It would take time, he says, to find a legal way back home.

In the meantime, you spend months living with your lawyer and his family: the Bolivars, compassionate people who offer you a home and several hot meals a day. They treat you like their son; their daughters treat you like their big brother. You see what a family could be. Parents can be kind and accepting, they can create comfort in their children's lives, they can value empathy over tradition. Venezuela, somehow, becomes a place of kindness and beauty.

The Bolivars accept you for who you are and treat you as an equal, never asking for anything in return. They bring you to family parties and include you on family trips. You vow to return one day in order to thank the Bolivars properly. You had expected to be in Venezuela for three days, but the months drag on.

The burial is excruciating, the women stay back and the men take to the front of the line. Custom stipulates that the immediate male family members are the ones who have the honor of beginning the burial process. As the Imam recites the Qur'an, the casket reaches its final resting spot. "Give me that shovel," you demand from a man you've never even seen. "He was my dad, not yours." The man surrenders the shovel and backs away for fear of catching the gay disease. "How dare you pick up my shovel," you think to yourself as you glare at him. No one says a word and the family tolerates your presence as the casket is lowered. Tears silently run down your face as you bury your father. Every move you make is tracked by the eyes of everyone around you. "I deserve to be here," you think to yourself as you watch the community hug your brother and offer prayers of healing.

After the casket is buried, you kneel to the ground, grab some dirt from the pile and run it through your fingers. No one else matters, you are alone and pray silently, you pray to Allah, asking him to forgive those that are ignorant. You ignore the presence of your entire family. "I forgive you," you whisper to the grave. Getting up, you dust yourself off, hold your head high, and walk away. Gina wasn't allowed to be near the men during the burial so she had stayed back, but now you focus on her as you walk away. She is so much taller than most of those puny men, almost my height. You feel the weight of their glances behind you, their eyes fixed on you. "Focus on Gina— don't give them what they want— focus on Gina— don't turn around just focus on Gina."

Near the end of your fifth month, the Consul General informs you that you will be one of a handful of people around the world to be granted a Hu-

manitarian Parole Visa: it guarantees one year of residence with protection against deportation, but no authorization to work. When you return to the embassy to collect your visa, the Consul General warns you that your life upon returning would not be the same. In particular, you would have no family to support you. Your lawyer informs you that during those months in Venezuela, your parents had bribed the local authorities to drop all charges and returned to the United States. You thank him, nonetheless, and promise that you would do nothing but great things back home. You return to the U.S. using a plane ticket purchased by friends.

The funeral was the last time you would see your family. It's time to close the chapter on that toxic relationship and begin to focus on your own healing. It no longer matters to you if they thought it was your fault that your father was gone. It no longer matters how ridiculous it sounds that his utter shame for a gay son could cause him to keel over and die. It no longer matters what these people thought at all— you forgive them for being so narrow minded. It's time to focus on the Samer you will become. You don't want another person to ever go through what you went through. You are going to position yourself in the world in a capacity where you can create change for the better. You don't want another young kid to be ripped out of innocence and plunged into a world of betrayal and survival— a dark world no one deserves to know. It's time to get started.

You become an activist. By the winter of 2016, you're giving a speech to hundreds of people on a freezing cold day in Chicago, your fur hat twice the size of your head. America needs to accept more Syrian refugees into our country, you say. These people aren't vagabonds and thieves. They aren't terrorists and violent woman-beaters—they're scared and in need of a chance to begin anew. You light candles and sing songs in Hebrew, Arabic, and English with the crowd. A couple camera crews show up and you make sure to speak louder and enunciate. "Chicago stands with refugees!" you yell into the crowd and they respond, chanting those words over and over.

When someone is utterly desperate and hope avails them at every turn, they stretch out their arms as far as they can and plead for a helping hand, any helping hand. They are drowning— they only need something to grab onto in order to live. You would know; you nearly drowned in that sea yourself. You have seen the worst that humanity has to offer, but you have also seen the best. You wouldn't be here if it weren't for the kindness of others.

You apply to colleges. You get into one of the best in the nation. You move to New York, build a life, and all of a sudden it's the first morning of classes of your senior year. You're the first person in class, like always. You sit at the front of the classroom so that you don't miss a word. This school challenges you to your core, and you often find yourself deconstructing and reconstructing your own stances on morality and justice to better understand them. At this prestigious university, you learn the great Why behind the decisions that affect our communities large and small.

It's also a place where rich kids come to gloat. A student walks in loudly, a large Starbucks cup in his hand and the floral print scarf around his neck, about which he's told us several times is the latest trend in Milan right now. Class doesn't start for ten more minutes. He's complaining about his parents, they've been two days late in sending him his allowance. He looks at you and says, "Parents can be so cruel." You scrunch your face and manage to churn out a sympathetic smile and nod.

My Other Name Is Morales Which Is Pronounced *Morales*

Milwaukee, WI

JENNIFER MORALES

My other name is Morales which is pronounced *Morales*.
Morales is the same as *Morales*, except *Morales* holds the heartbreak.
Mora is a mulberry and *moral* is the tree or shrub.
Morales are the árboles lined up in a regimented Spanish grove,
grown in conscripted soil
to feed the worms
that make the nests
that are spun into thread
that is woven and sold, woven and sold,
an unfurling tapestry of brown hands,
Mexican *indio* palms and Chinese peasant fingers.

Morales is pronounced with the berry still in it,
juicy and purple,
with a lithe green stem threaded through,
a sea creature's undulating spine.
Morales draws up water
from the earth and down from the sky,
staining the day,
offering absolution to no one.

ᏗᎶᏏᏆᎠᎩ ᏗᏕᏪᎰᏆᎠᎩ ᏡᏏᏕᏋ

Digital Talking Leaves

Oklahoma City, OK

PATRICK DEL PERCIO

~ ᎨᏬ ~

She glances over at my bag
The one with the enamel rainbow pin attached to it
My nerves begin to overcome me
ᎠᏟᎷᎫ ᏓᏍᏛ ᎣᏆᏩᏒT
A gentle smile across her face
I repeat for clarification
ᎠᏟᎷᎫ ᏓᏍᏛ ᎣᏆᏩᏒT
My face lights up
A river of warmth washes over me
My discomfort dissipates
Bursting with pride

~ ᎳᏞ ~

ᎠᏫC ᎠᏗᎭ
These words taste of sweet nectar
Send a warm tingle down my spine
That specific sensation you feel when hugging a friend you haven't seen in
a while
ᎠᏫC ᎠᏗᎭ
Neither here Neither there
In the middle
ᎠᏫC ᎠᏗᎭ
Creates a world for us to love without limits
A world in which we can live exactly as ourselves
ᎠᏫC ᎠᏗᎭ
A homecoming

~ KT ~

Mornings turn to afternoons as each word brings more and more laughter
ᎢᏳ ᏂᎭᏛᏉ ᏔᏥᏆᏫᎩ
I laugh more in Cherokee than I do in English
I say to my friend
She nods her head in agreement
Throws her head back, chuckling
ᎢᏳ ᏂᎭᏛᏉ ᏔᏥᏆᏫᎩ
Reminiscing about the many things her grandpa and grandma used to say
ᎢᏳ ᏂᎭᏛᏉ ᏔᏥᏆᏫᎩ
This brings more laughter and ear to ear smiles
Our conversations never quite long enough
Until tomorrow tomorrow tomorrow
ᏒᎦᏛᎢ ᏒᎦᏛᎢ ᏒᎦᏛᎢ

~ ᏅᎩ ~

I am fourteen years old
September leaves twirl past the window on their way to the lawn
I press the computer to life
Logging into an online Cherokee language world
This will soon become my favorite time of the day
Our teacher fills this space with humor and so many stories
My brain clings to every word
Every phrase
Every sound
A language unfamiliar to my ears
Familiar to heart in ways for which I didn't yet have the words

~ ᎯᏍᎩ ~

I write the word in phonetics first
I need to see all the sounds
Then I try my hand at writing in syllabary
My fingers trace across the pocket-sized syllabary chart
Shaky at first unsure of the pen stroke
Finally I translate the word into English
ᎣᏍᏓ ᎣᏍᏓ ᎣᏍᏓ
O-s-da O-s-da O-s-da
I repeat the syllables slowly then put them together
Good good good

~ ᎨᏓᎵ ~

It's a sweltering day in August
The middle of an intense Oklahoma summer
Rummaging through my belongings
Trying to acclimate to new surroundings
Escaping the scorching heat that awaits me outside
I open one box then another
There must be about 20 notebooks here
I flip to a special page
Here, with the guidance of my mentor
I separate the verb by their sounds
He has me do this so I will understand
Each syllable has a tone
Each syllable has a meaning
I put them together in such a way that I paint a whole story in my mind

~ ᏍᏛᏗᏫᏯ ~

Over under Over under
With each new row she tells me a new word
Over under Over under
She tells me never forget
Over under Over under
I make sure there are no spaces in the bottom
Over under Over under
I repeat the syllables slowly then pick up the pace
Over under over under
I pull tight tight tight
Over under Over under
Careful so as not to let any sound fall out
Over under Over under
Ꮮ ᏔᏆᎿᏩ ᏙᏣᎬᎨᎣᏍ
Over under Over under
I know, she says

~ ᏣᏂᏯ ~

ᎫᏍᏫᎾᏍᎫᏔ
Our ancestors breathe life into these walls
ᏴᏍᏍᏯ

Here we gather to learn, dance, love, mourn, and rejoice
ᏗᏍᏪᎾᏍᎫᎢ
It takes a community to stoke the fire of our language
ᏍᏏᏉ
We all need each other in order to grow
ᏗᏍᏪᎾᏍᎫᎢ
Elders say ᏣᏯ ᏍᎤᎯᎠᏍᏗ is a gift directly from ᎤᏓᏂᏎᎤᎠ
ᏍᏏᏉ
It takes dedication dedication dedication
ᏗᏍᏪᎾᏍᎫᎢ
So we continue to breathe life into these words and songs, wherever we are
ᏍᏏᏉ
A space for family whom I have yet to meet
ᏗᏍᏪᎾᏍᎫᎢ

A Tale of Three Seasons:
Black Midwestern Lesbian Lineages

Cleveland, OH

JASMINE BURNETT

My maternal grandmother's sister, my great aunt Betty showed me the meaning of my name in her life's example well before I was aware of Audre Lorde's, *"Zami"* because, like me, she was a Black midwestern lesbian woman. I came out to my mother at 19 years old, but my Aunt Betty never "officially" came out. She simply lived and allowed you to arrive at your own decisions about how you thought she was living her life. She wasn't gonna volunteer shit about herself and dared you to ask her outright.

As a young child, intimacies of her life were not treated as a matter of simple fact in our family like they did with everyone else who was in a heterosexual relationship, and brought their significant other home for events and holidays. This was actually dictated to me in a way that I knew something was up, I just didn't know what. The suggestive insights into her life were communicated through their leering eyes, hushed tones and chuckles of other adults. All I knew was every Christmas we celebrated at my grandmother's house, and I would get so excited knowing that my Great Grandmother along with Aunt Betty and cousin Annie would make the two-hour drive from Dayton, Ohio to my hometown Anderson, Indiana. Aunt Betty and cousin Annie always slept in the same bed at my grandparents house in the living room on the pull-out couch. I noticed this when I was about three-years-old and thought it was completely normal because my cousin Bubbles and I took baths together and slept in the same bed. I thought that's what all cousins do. It didn't alarm me that Aunt Betty and cousin Annie shared a bed even though I knew they had separate bedrooms at their house.

Season 1: Childhood Summers

It was the summer of 1988, I was 8 years old and Aunt Betty asked if me and Bubbles could spend the summer in Dayton and stay at her and cousin Annie's house. After talking with my mother and Bubbles' dad, my uncle they decided we could go and I remember being so damn excited! The only time our family visited Dayton was for Thanksgiving at my great grandmother's house. Her house wasn't nearly as interesting as Aunt Betty's even though she did operate a home-based salon in her basement for nearly 40 years from the late 1930's when she and my great grandfather migrated from Carrollton, GA in the early 1980s, so I thought that everyone's grandmother had a home based business. In fact, my grandmother was a barber and her barbershop was connected to our family's home.

I loved visiting Aunt Betty. Her house was small and tidy, yet held an air of mystery and wonder. First of all, she had a king sized waterbed, which in the heyday of waterbeds was like purchasing a brand new Cadillac from the showroom floor. Having a waterbed indicated flash, leisure and wealth. It could have also been the overwhelming fragrance of cedar chips and moth balls that permeated her home, or it may have even been the walls of squared mirrors that so many families had in the 1980's and the ability to look at yourself from multiple spaces in her living room. I remember how those mirrors gave me Bruce Lee, "Fists of Fury" vibes, where he had to sense where the attack was coming from in the room of mirrors. Aunt Betty had three modes of transportation. A two-door 1987 Buick Riviera that had cream paint with a chocolate brown top and peanut butter colored leather seats, a minivan that had the profile of queen Nefertiti engraved in color on the van running board and a camper that she took on her fishing trips. I loved that she had a portable toilet in that van! Needless to say, I was intrigued. This would be my first summer away from home in another state.

Before Bubbles and I were driven to our summer vacation destination, we were given a good talking to by all of my maternal aunts, uncle and grandfather. The younger aunts who were in their 20's at the time cautioned me and Bubbles to watch for anything "funny" that might go on at Aunt Betty's house. The mystery and wonder I held about her house was only enhanced from the story my aunts told me. When they were little and visited Aunt Betty, they said she and cousin Annie had "His & Her" towels in the bathroom. When they noticed the towels, they asked my grandmother how was cousin Annie "blood-related" to us and she told them, "Annie is a family member by marriage of some cousins in the South." As an adult reflecting on my childhood, I realize that my grandmother, who Bubbles and I affectionately called Mamae, was slick with how she dished out that information. She was vague but nothing she said was untrue. What I knew for sure was that nothing that I was "forewarned of" when I was a child, or as I am reminiscing on it as an adult scared me in the least bit.

I don't remember much about the drive to Dayton, but I do remember arriving at Aunt Betty and cousin Annie's house. I will never forget that house, it was a bungalow style white house with black shutters, two bedrooms, one bathroom, livingroom, kitchen and a semi-finished basement with a half bath. Although her home was not larger than about 700 square feet it felt like a mansion to me and the dollhouse I never had. We put our bags away in cousin Annie's room and got settled in with a proper tour of the house. This included where we would be sleeping, complete with things we were warned not to touch and rooms to not enter without knocking. Cousin Annie then took us on a tour of their short block in the neighborhood and introduced us to kids who became our friends that summer and the candy lady across the street with the delicious ice cups of multiple sugary flavors. That first night, Aunt Betty took us to our first "Drive-In" movie to see Eddie Murphy's, *"Coming To America."* She was a retired government clerk and cousin Annie worked for a local family-owned hardware store. Sometimes she would take me and Bubbles to work with her. I knew that it was going to be a magical summer.

There was one day when Aunt Betty and cousin Annie were encouraging us to go outside and play but we decided it was too damn hot and we wanted to watch TV on their nice floor model television. I will never forget laying on my stomach on the red shag carpet watching the 1943 American musical, *"Stormy Weather"* starring Lena Horne. It was my first time watching that film and the first I had ever seen Black characters featured so regal and beautiful in a black and white film. I was engrossed till the very end when I happened to see cousin Annie scurry from Aunt Betty's room wrapped in a white sheet and from what I could tell, not much else underneath. Then, Aunt Betty called my name and told me to come here. I looked at Bubbles and mouthed, *"bitch, why didn't she call you?"* She mouthed and replied, *"bitch, I don't know but you better go see what she wants!"* Aunt Betty called for me again, and I stalled and asked, *"do you want me to bring you something to drink?"* She said, *"no girl, just come here."* I went to her room, stepping very slowly. Somehow, I knew I was going to see something on the other side of that door that would answer so many questions for me.

My stomach flipped as I knocked on her bedroom door, and she told me to come in. As I walked in, her long graceful body was stretched out across her king sized waterbed and she was wearing a white collared buttoned shirt and was covered in her bedding from the waist down. Such a mystery, she was. With a smile of warmth and a look in her eyes that told me all that I needed to know about what she was feeling in that moment, she asked, *"did you like the movie?"* I replied, *"yes, that woman who was singing was so pretty. She looks like you in your old pictures."* To which she said, *"just because me and Lena Horne are light-skinned and both have wavy hair doesn't mean we look alike, child."* I just stood there, still in disbelief about what she was revealing to me in all of my 8 year old intuition. Aunt Betty laughed and said, *"well I'm glad you liked the movie."* As I walked back out to the living room and closed her bedroom door certain that I had been let in on the secret of all secrets, I mouthed to myself, *"now I know, Aunt Annie and cousin Annie are together."* As I think back to what "knowing" at that moment meant to me, I felt mature beyond my years and proud that she trusted me and knew me well enough to know that I could hold this information about her life.

The sun was going down, cousin Annie gave us an afternoon snack and finally Bubbles and I went back outside to play. Every weekend, Bubbles and I would fulfill one of our family's rites of passage and go to my great grandmother's house on Saturday to attend church on Sunday, and so that Aunt Betty could entertain her friends. As the summer was coming to a close, there was one weekend that we stayed at Aunt Betty's house. Her friends—all women—were filing in from the back door, which led to the kitchen and a door to the stairs of her basement. They all came in adorned in their gold jewelry, various hairstyles, some dawning sunglasses and shag Jherri curls and others with their beautiful faces made up, looking like Norma Jean Robinson and Luci Martin of 1970's group Chic on the album cover of their greatest hits. Aunt Betty's friends were just as mysterious as she was and I wanted to watch them and take them in, but I was a child and had to go to bed, but there was no way that I was going to sleep. That night I heard their muffled voices, interspersed with cackles and smelled cigarette smoke wafting from the vents. I wanted to know what they were talking about. I wanted to hang out with her friends. I would have the opportunity in a later season.

Season 2: The Mysteries and Changes of the Fall

The years passed of Aunt Betty and cousin Annie coming to Indiana for Christmas and our family in Indiana driving to Dayton for Thanksgiving. Life moved on and the elders in our family, my Grandmother "Mamae", grandfather and great grandmother had transitioned. In the fall of 2003, when I was 24 years old I learned that Aunt Betty had been diagnosed with an advanced stage of lung cancer. She smoked cigarettes all of my life which meant by this particular year, she had been smoking for at least 24 years and many more before that. When I learned how ill she was, I wanted to be with her and help out cousin Annie, whom I had then started to call Aunt Annie.

By this time, I had been "out" to my family for a few years. My mother had just started talking to me again after not talking to me for three years because I was a lesbian. I was also in my first long term relationship after having two previously failed relationships with other women. I was blossoming in my lesbian identity and wanted to spend time with the women who helped shape my understanding of this life of loving women and loving myself.

Aunt Betty was hospitalized quite a bit the late summer and early fall of that year. We were lucky that she was able to make her final holiday trip to Indiana on Thanksgiving. I remember her being unusually quiet and deeply reflective her entire visit. My then-girlfriend and I made a point to extend love and care to Aunt Betty and Aunt Annie, so we took a trip to Dayton, to spend the weekend with them. This was a trip where I remembered the drive there because Aunt Betty sent me a letter with a map from Indianapolis directly to her house. It was the sweetest thing I had ever received in the mail.

When we arrived, Aunt Betty was in frail health but so happy to see us. She spent most of the time laid out on her sofa and struggling to breathe. What let me know she was still with us was when I flat out asked her if she and Aunt Annie were lesbian lovers. She had NEVER shared that she was a lesbian to our family and I felt because I was out that she would tell me and confirm it once and for all. The conversation went something like this:

"Aunt Betty, are you a lesbian?"

She said, "Ohh girl you've got some nerve asking me that question flat out!"

I became nervous and confused, I wasn't sure if I upset her or if she was teasing me. Some moments passed where she let me sit in the stew of my question to her, I felt hot, faint, strange and weak. The last thing I wanted to do was offend her.

Then, she just busted out laughing and said, "Annie, can you believe this child just asked us if we were L E S B I A N S?! Woo, the children got some guts these days."

Aunt Annie said, "Say what Betty? I don't know what we are! Are we L E S B I A N S?"

Boy did they have a good laugh on my account. What I didn't know then is that they came of age during a time when homosexuality was expressed at home only, or in the company of trusted friends—never family. Given my experience with telling my family and how hurtful that was for me, even in the 1990s, I understood why Aunt Betty didn't go through the trouble of telling them.

Born in 1931, Aunt Betty came of age as a young woman during the Cold War. Government tensions with the Soviet Union were high. The McCarthy Hearings were a government crusade that was executing "witch hunts" for people who they deemed dangerous, which have always included homosexuals and Black people. The privacy and discretion that gay and lesbian folks coveted at that time literally saved their lives, livelihoods, and protected them from imprisonment. It was a heavy time to be anything other than a white heterosexual man.

When I asked Aunt Betty why she never married, she said, *"Girl, ain't nothing a man can do for me that I can't do for myself. I wasn't gonna have no man trying to control my money and beat me upside my head if I didn't give it to him. Meanwhile he out here giving my money to another bitch in the streets. Nope, the answer was always going to be no."* Though she painted a bleak picture of her confidence in men, she shared stories of how she captured the attention of men with her butterscotch skin, wavy bobbed hair parted on the side framing the angles of her face to perfection, a red lip dawning a smile that was coy and mischievous while carrying the slender gait and height of a six foot tall goddess. Aunt Betty received three proposals from men in her younger years and gave them a firm "no" every time at the dismay of her mother who couldn't understand why she didn't, *"want a man to marry."*

There was a curious dynamic about Aunt Betty in my family. On one hand they acknowledged that she was not into men, but didn't accept that she was a lesbian who never identified herself as such in our family. There was always tension about the discussion of Aunt Betty's sexuality. I later learned from my mother that Aunt Betty never received the respect she deserved from her mother about who she loved and the choices she made for her life. It was a situation of a loud silence.

One sweet story that Aunt Betty did share with me on one of my visits to Dayton when she was in the hospital was how she courted Aunt Annie. December 1967 Dionne Warwick released her hit song, *"I Say A Little Prayer,"* released again a year later by Aretha Franklin. Every morning during the spring and summer of 1968, Aunt Betty would park outside of Aunt Annie's apartment in her candy red drop top Chevrolet Camaro with the black rag top with black leather interior and play that song for her before pulling off to start her day. That was the sweetest story she shared with me about their love for each other. One year later, Aunt Annie moved in with Aunt Betty and they began their lives together.

There came a point in Aunt Betty's illness where she could no longer travel to Indiana and Aunt Annie would come on her own. On one of those trips, Aunt Annie told my aunts and uncles that she and Aunt Betty were lovers and had been together for 35 years. Her exact words were, *"Betty isn't doing well with her health and by now y'all know I am not your cousin. Me and your Aunt Betty been together since all of y'all we're little and I'm going to be there till the end."* I held Aunt Annie's hand as she shared this detail about her life with my family. My heart eased into my throat as I felt her fear through her trembling body and sweaty palms. My mother and her sisters were shocked at how forthright Aunt Annie was about the truth they had been speculating about for so many years. They didn't particularly appreciate it even though they were respectful of Aunt Annie who they still called, cousin Ann. After Aunt Annie drove back to Dayton, the conversation was especially difficult with one of my aunts she said, *"so what they've been together, what's that supposed to mean!"*

The following spring and summer of 2004, since I was spending quite a bit of time driving from Indianapolis to Dayton to check on Aunt Betty and Aunt Annie, I met those friends I saw going into Aunt Betty's basement that first summer I spent at her house! During one of my visits, we went to one of their longtime friend's houses who I'll call Barb. When I walked in, I knew I was the youngest person there and was instantly taken back by the number of card tables in this cozy basement, where at least 25 lesbians were playing cards, eating, smoking cigarettes and talking cash money shit. I sat at a table with a woman who was a "high femme," absolutely in her 60s, and so beautiful. She said, *"I want to play four hands with the young woman with the beautiful smile."* Of course, I blushed and played my four hands of spades while she gently and flirtatiously dog walked me in this game and told me what cards were in my hand and what I was going to play next.

I met some of their friends who all called Aunt Betty "Pops" and Aunt Annie "Moms." They shared how Aunt Betty's basement was the safest place for them to be with each other and their ladies in public. One friend shared, *"It was the early 70's, I was 19 years old, had just come out and was lost. Pops brought me into her home and talked with me about women and how to move through this life with a woman. Hell, I kissed my first crush in her basement.* "What I had learned was Aunt Betty had an informal after-hours spot for Black lesbian women in the basement of her house from the late 1950s to the late 1980s. I was floored and awestruck. In that moment, I knew why her house and the basement in particular held so much allure, curiosity and fascination for me.

The more I visited Aunt Betty and Aunt Annie that summer, the more I visited with their friends and learned things about Aunt Betty that she never shared with the rest of our family. Much like when I visited my first summer as a child, sharing in her life made me feel mature, special, honored, privileged and righteously defiant in my family. Stories of long distance road trips where she and her friends caravanned before cell phones to make sure everyone was safe. That she had a bowling league with her friends called J.U.G.S. or "Just Us GirlS," that met weekly to bowl and build community with each other. And, her infamous fishing trips where they would hitch tents and set up trailers for a week in the wilderness. I can't even imagine the laughter and memories of sharing a campsite with a group of 20 or more Black lesbian womyn. Their stories of experiences with Aunt Betty and Aunt Annie sounded like the paradise I hoped my life would become one day.

As the summer turned into early fall, Aunt Betty was getting more ill. There were times where she would be exhausted after a procedure and I would visit her in the hospital to hold her hand and watch her sleep. Eventually, Aunt Betty needed to be transferred to a hospice. I was there the day she was transferred and followed behind the ambulance. The sun was shining and it was a beautiful day. As they were wheeling Aunt Betty into the facility, I saw her last bask in the sun and the smile that visited her lips from its warmth.

Early in the morning on September 8, 2004 Aunt Betty passed away in her sleep. I was in Dayton with Aunt Annie when she received the call from the hospice and I will never forget the wail of her sorrow. She was so devastated and simply could not handle seeing Aunt Betty without life in her body. Since Aunt Betty wanted to be cremated, someone needed to view her body before and so, I drove to the hospice. It was a rainy morning, and I was the last person who had the honor of seeing her beautiful lifeless body before it was processed in cremation. I wept as I kissed her check, laid my ear to her chest, stared at her peaceful face as I ran my fingers through her gorgeous hair and left.

My family's reaction to Aunt Annie was equally as traumatic as losing Aunt Betty. Before making funeral arrangements, my family drove a huge

16-foot Ryder truck to Dayton to clear out Aunt Betty and Aunt Annie's house. Mind you, Aunt Annie still lived there.

Before my family arrived with the truck, Aunt Annie shared with me that Aunt Betty wanted her to get rid of all of the film, photographs, letters and evidence of their relationship. No one would ever lay eyes on it except them. I supported Aunt Annie keeping the details of their lives together sacred by helping her destroy or throw away what was left of it. That was utterly devastating.

Aunt Annie's birthday was a little over a month after Aunt Betty passed away. I connected with her friends to arrange a surprise party for her 73rd birthday to be hosted by me and my then girlfriend at our home in Indianapolis, Indiana. It was a special party and we had a ball. It was as if I got a taste of what it might have been like in Aunt Betty's basement all those years ago. There was dancing, drinking, eating, celebration, arguing, tears and more dancing. I am thankful to have the images from that special night after being forced to toss out so many other memories to honor Aunt Betty's final wishes. My family wasn't supportive of me continuing a relationship with Aunt Annie and I eventually moved away from Indiana and ended my relationship with my then-girlfriend to pursue a life in California. When I tried to re-establish contact with Aunt Annie, she said it was too difficult to be connected to anyone in our family, including me.

Season 3: Springtime with Aunt Betty's Basement on Facebook

I wanted to create memories of Aunt Betty beyond the bitterness that tainted my spirit from the way my family treated Aunt Annie. I felt so powerless to stop them from essentially running through Aunt Betty's house and taking anything they felt they deserved. Deaths in a family reveal the nature of the relationships beneath the surface and the bitter taste that was left in my mouth after my family handled Aunt Annie in such an abrasive and heartless way was more than I could handle. It was 2009, I was living in Los Angeles, single, entering my 30's and ready to enhance my learning with and in service of Black lesbian women. I was inspired by reading things Felice Newman's landmark book, *The Whole Lesbian Sex Book: A Passionate Guide For All Of Us (2004)*, Nick Karras' book, *"Petals,"* a series of 48 deliciously photographed sepia toned pictures of vulvas, and a special thanks to all of the beautiful women I met and connected with in L.A. The failed relationship with Aunt Annie left a scar on my heart that aches like the initial blow every time I think about it. I needed an outlet to hold their legacy of community, support and care for each other and transform it from the basement into "real time, real talk" conversation. I was encouraged to create conversations among Black lesbian women through an online platform I created called Aunt Betty's Basement

The motto of, Aunt Betty's Basement is, *"Pussy Power "* *which* reflects self knowledge about one's health and pleasure connected with the physical and emotional awareness of others. The online format was reflected in conversations about trauma, hygiene, discussion about sexual preferences and tips along with any number of things that Black and multi-racial lesbians and queer womyn were curious about. I craved a community without physical boundaries or conversational limitations about sex and eroticism so I also held, "Positive Pussy Parties" which operated a lot like the feminist consciousness-raising circles except they were more femme and queer. These spaces were the first time many of the women and folks who attended ever talked about their trauma, desires and aspirations for their erotic lives out loud. It is as if Black women and femmes are not allowed to believe that the pleasure we desire is available to us. This digital community hosted over 1,000 members and created a space for us to exist in the realities of our lives and be able to ask questions that many people did not have access to in their communities. This space was introduced as a way to center the lives and experiences of cisgender Black lesbian womyn because as the LGBTQAI+ lexicon became more expansive, so did the fluidity of sexual identities and gender expressions. I wanted to ensure that Black lesbian identities did not become absorbed, denied, eliminated and essentially gentrified within the broader community. I wanted a space for us to recognize ourselves in the traditions of Ruth Ellis a Black lesbian woman patron saint from Detroit, MI who had a "safe house" for LGBTQ folks in the 1950s, or the Black lesbian social group that I was a member of Indy Soul Sistahs, which held bi-weekly brunches and social spaces in Indianapolis, IN or the long gone, "Lesbian Bars" or "Women-only" nights at clubs.

After over 20 years of being an out Black lesbian woman, I have also turned some corners in my family where I once was consumed with their acceptance of me, now I know whether or not that happens, I am living the life that honors my truest expression. Also, my younger family members give me hope that what I experienced coming out—with my mother not talking to me for three years and my extended family support being consistent and positive for some, and unpredictable and messy for others—

demonstrates to me that my experience of being isolated showed my family a better way to be and overcome their homophobia. I truly believe that my coming out healed my Aunt Betty's trauma of living her life in my family as a closeted Black lesbian and broke a cycle of intergenerational trauma for the future of our family. My mother passed away February 2018 and days before she passed, we reconciled our years of unaddressed harm from my coming out. In many ways, my family has come full circle about gender and sexuality. It's not perfect by far, but I do see the evolution as Aunt Betty was the trailblazer, me as the bridge generation and now the younger queers in my family have a level of care, love and respect that we should all have when we live in the truth of our lives.

Unfortunately the circle was never quite complete with my relationship with Aunt Annie after I learned she passed away October 2015 from Alzheimer's disease. I often wonder if the pain of remembering what her life was with Aunt Betty and grieving her relationship with our family took her memory away as a way to endure life as it was, and not as she remembered it. Unfortunately, I will never have the opportunity to know in her own voice.

Barbara Smith said in an issue of the lesbian feminist literary magazine *Conditions* published in 1979, the year I was born: "As Black women, as Lesbians and feminists there is no guarantee that our lives will ever be looked at with the kind of respect given to certain people from other races, sexes or classes. There is singularly no guarantee that we or our movement will survive long enough to become safely historical. We must document ourselves now."

Black lesbian womyn, we deserve everything our ancestors dreamt for us and everything we could ever vision and never imagine for ourselves. For as long as I have life on this earth, it is my righteous charge and profound honor to document our lives, lineages and experiences.

CONTRIBUTORS

Kemi Alabi is the author of *The Lion Tamer's Daughter*. Their poetry and essays have been published in *Boston Review*, *The Break Beat Poets Vol. 2* and elsewhere. Kemi is the Cultural Strategy Director of Forward Together, and lives in Chicago, IL.

Samuel Autman's "Wonder Boys" was adapted into the award-winning short film "A Long Walk," available at www.samuelautman.com. His other essays have appeared in *The Kept Secret: The Half-Truth in Nonfiction*, *Brevity* and *The St. Louis Anthology*.

Neema Avashia is an 8th grade Civics teacher in the Boston Public Schools, where she has taught for the last 16 years. She grew up in Cross Lanes, WV, in the heart of the Chemical Valley.

Lars Avis (he/him) is a poet, musician, and English Publishing Studies major at Illinois State University. He was born in and (mostly) raised around Peoria, IL, also living in Georgia and England. Lars's poetry has been published in Bluffs Literary Magazine, Broadside Literary Arts Journal and elsewhere.

Joss Barton is a writer, journalist, and spoken word performance artist exploring and documenting queer and trans* life, love, and liberation. Her work blends femme-fever dreams over the soundtrack of the American nightmare. She resides and writes in Saint Louis, Missouri.

Yasmin Bashir is a writer from Saint Louis, Missouri currently living in Chicago, Illinois. She is interested in spirituality and the body as it relates to black womanhood and feminist theory.

Jeffery Beam is the author of over 20 works of poetry including *The New Beautiful Tendons: Collected Queer Poems 1969-2012*, and *Spectral Pegasus / Dark Movements* with Welsh painter Clive Hicks-Jenkins.

Zach Benak, originally from Papillion, Nebraska, now lives, writes, and works in Chicago. His prose appears in GASHER, Crook and Folly, and The Paragon Journal.

Taylor Brorby is the author of *Crude: Poems*, and *Coming Alive: Action and Civil Disobedience*. He's a contributing editor at *North American Review*, and has received fellowships from the MacDowell Colony and the National Book Critics Circle.

Jasmine Burnett is a third generation Black Midwesterner, Lesbian and Feminist. These identities inform her passion as a cultural worker who uses pleasure, intimacy and naturism through storytelling.

River Coello (he/she/they) is an Ecuadorian-American and two-spirit multidisciplinary artist, whose writing and performance work explores human liminalities and temporalities. River's most recent writing project, *self/ser*, was published by Homie House Press.

Edward M. Cohen's novel, "$250,000," was published by Putnam's; his nonfiction books by Prima, Prentice-Hall, and Limelight Editions. His short story collection won the 2019 Awst Press Book Award and will be published later this year.

Brian Czyzyk is an MFA candidate at Purdue University, originally from Northern Michigan. His work has appeared in *Colorado Review*, *Nimrod*, and the *New Poetry from the Midwest 2019* anthology, among others.

Harmony Cox is one of the managing editors of the popular satire website The Belladonna. She hosts Story Club Columbus, frequently performs at local literary events, and her work has appeared in Narratively, McSweeneys, and elsewhere.

Gene Dawson, originally of Parnell, Iowa, first went out in drag in 1954. He is a longtime resident of St. Louis, Missouri.

Patrick Del Percio is of Cherokee, Italian, and Irish descent, grew up in northern Illinois and currently resides in Oklahoma City. He/They are faculty at the University of Oklahoma as a Cherokee language Instructor in the Department of Native American Studies.

Dominick Duda's work has appeared in *Black Market Lit*, *The Mill*, and elsewhere. He is a 2017 Pushcart Prize nominee and the 2015 recipient of the A.W. "Bud" Collins, Jr. Prize in Creative Writing.

Joanna Eleftheriou is the author of the essay collection *This Way Back*. She holds a PhD from the University of Missouri and a fellowship from the Virginia Center for the Creative Arts. She is an assistant professor of English at Christopher Newport University, and a contributing editor of *Assay: A Journal of Nonfiction Studies*.

Aaron Foley is a Detroit-based writer. He is the author of *How to Live in Detroit Without Being a Jackass* and the editor of *The Detroit Neighborhood Guidebook*.

Christopher Gonzalez is an ex-Clevelander living and writing in New York. His work appears in Little Fiction, The Nation, Best Small Fictions 2019, Lunch Ticket, Wasafiri, and elsewhere.

Stacy Grover is a transgender Appalachian essayist and translator from Carroll, Ohio. Her writing appears in Belt Publishing, HEArt Online Journal, InsideHigherEd and elsewhere. Find her at www.stacyjanegrover.com

Elizabeth Harper lives in Chicago where she hosts the Elizabeth's Crazy Little Thing open mic variety show, and writes for the Literate Ape website. Her books include *Love Songs from Psychopaths*, *A Mercenary Girdler*, and several chapbooks.

Jackie Hedeman's work has appeared in Electric Literature, The Best American Travel Writing 2017, Autostraddle, The Offing, and elsewhere. Find her on Twitter @JackieHedeman

Jessica Jacobs is the author of *Take Me with You, Pelvis with Distance*, winner of the New Mexico Book Award in Poetry and a finalist for the Lambda Literary Award, and more. She lives in Asheville, NC with her wife.

C.J. Janovy is a public radio and former alt-weekly journalist in Kansas City, Missouri, where she lives with her wife and two dogs. She is the author of *No Place Like Home: Lessons in Activism from LGBT Kansas*. Follow her on Twitter @cjjanovy.

Jessie Keary is a nonbinary writer from Missouri with a BA in creative writing from DePaul University. You can follow Jessie on Twitter and Instagram—@jessiekeary

Owen Keehnen has written several fiction and nonfiction books. He was a cofounder of the Legacy Project and is currently working to make AIDS Garden Chicago a reality. He was inducted into the Chicago LGBT Hall of Fame in 2011.

River Ian Kerstetter is a queer transfeminine artist, writer, and educator of Onʌyotaʼa:ka (Wisconsin Oneida) and European-American heritage, who grew up in occupied Pueblo lands (Central New Mexico) and now lives and works in occupied Odawa, Ojibwe, and Potawatomi lands (Chicago). Her work reflects her search for community and connection in a post-colonial world where queer, trans, and Indigenous people fight to be seen and safe every day.

Doug Kiel is a citizen of the Oneida Nation and identifies as Two-Spirit. He is an Assistant Professor in the Department of History and the Alice Kaplan Institute for the Humanities at Northwestern University. He is from Wisconsin, and now lives in Chicago.

Jocelyn Krueger is a multidisciplinary artist with degrees from the University of Iowa and an MFA from Indiana State University. Jocelyn lives in Terre Haute with her wife and children, cats, books and garden.

Nichole Lohrman-Novak is a high school English teacher in a small, urban district. She and her wife, Megan, live in Newark, Ohio with their cat, Gavyn, and dog, Willow.

Raymond Luczak is the author and editor of 22 books, including *Flannelwood* and *Among the Leaves: Queer Male Poets on the Midwestern Experience*. He lives in Minneapolis, Minnesota.

Ka "Oskar" Ly is a Hmong French-American artist and cultural producer based in Saint Paul, MN. Their work centers on confronting Hmong aesthetics, uplifting abundant celebration of their communities, and willing previously unimaginable possibilities into undeniable existence.

K. Ann MacNeil lives in Manhattan, but has traveled to the Midwest to visit her chosen family for thirty years. Her work appears in *This Assignment is So Gay: LGBTIQ Poets on the Art of Teaching*, with work forthcoming in *Closet Cases: Queers on What We Wear*.

Mary Maxfield questions place, technology, and LGBTQQIA+ community formation through both creative writing and academic scholarship. Mary's work has been featured in *Feminist Media Studies, Frontiers: A Journal of Women Studies,* and elsewhere.

Gabe Montesanti has an MFA from Washington University in St. Louis and teaches creative writing at the Missouri Eastern Correctional Center. Her first book, a roller derby memoir, is forthcoming. Other work can be found at *Brevity, Creative Nonfiction Magazine*, and *The Offing*.

Jennifer Morales is a Wisconsin-based poet, fiction writer, and performance artist whose work wrestles with gender, identity, complicity, and harm. Jennifer's book, *Meet Me Halfway*, a short story collection about life in hyper-segregated Milwaukee, was Wisconsin Center for the Book's 2016 "Book of the Year."

Kalene Nisly is a creative and therapist living on the plains of Kansas. She lives in an old home with her partner, and a small band of children and animals.

Andriy Partykevich is originally from Chicago, was ordained in the Ukrainian Orthodox Church of the USA and served in parishes for 23 years. By his own choice, Andriy no longer serves as an active priest and lives in Florida with his husband.

Robert L. Patrick, born in Wurzburg, Germany and raised in Rapid City, South Dakota, lives in Southern California with his life-partner of 38 years. His work has appeared in the online literary journals, *Chelsea Station Magazine* and *Bull Men's Fiction*.

Kay Patterson is Rust Belt born and bred, raised in Toledo, Ohio, and educated at Michigan State University. She is part of an active writing community in her adopted hometown Buffalo, New York.

Angela Pupino grew up in Ohio's Mahoning Valley where she became a bisexual Christian. She has written about her life in the Rust Belt for *CNN* and *The Nation* and hopes to one day be ordained in the United Methodist Church.

Kai Minosh Pyle is a Métis and Sault Ste. Marie Nishnaabe Two-Spirit writer originally from Green Bay and currently living on the Dakota people's homelands in Bde Ota Othunwe (Minneapolis, Minnesota). Their book of Anishinaabemowin and Michif-language poetry, AANAWI GO, was published in January 2020.

Samer Hassan Saleh is a current student at Columbia University New York City. He is a social justice activist and current Policy and Advocacy Fellow with Young Invincibles.

Michael Schreiber's debut book, *One-Man Show: The Life and Art of Bernard Perlin*, was named a Stonewall Honor Book by the American Library Association, and is being adapted into a feature-length film.

Sharon Seithel is a lifelong Missourian, born in Cape Girardeau, . She currently resides in St. Louis with her wife Carol and their three dogs. She recently retired from a career in technology and dreams of becoming a writer, activist and amateur historian.

L.S. Quinn is an artist and activist. She founded and operates The Reading Room CLE, a nonprofit bookstore that offers literary and literacy programs in Cleveland, Ohio.

José Quiñones is a native Chicagoan who graduated from DePaul University. Currently working in fashion, Jose always finds time to write and find good places for coffee

Sarah Sala is the author of *Devils' Lake*, founder of the free poetry workshop, Office Hours, and Assistant Poetry Editor at the *Bellevue Literary Review*. Visit her at sarahsala.com and @sarahmsala.

James Schwartz is a poet, slam performer, and author of five poetry collections including The Literary Party: Growing Up Gay and Amish in America. Follow him on Twitter at @queeraspoetry.

Gregg Shapiro is the author of seven books including the 2019 chapbooks, *Sunshine State* and *More Poems About Buildings and Food*. Shapiro lives in Fort Lauderdale, Florida with his husband Rick and their dog Coco.

Joel Showalter's poems appear in *The Carolina Quarter*, *The Christian Century*, and elsewhere. He's originally from Indiana, but lives now with his husband in Columbus, Ohio, where he's the editorial director at a marketing agency.

Carmen Smith, originally from Peoria, Illinois, now lives in Colorado Springs, CO in the tiny house she built with her wonderful wife, Elise.

Robyn Steely's writing has appeared in *Front Porch* and *Culinate*. Her poem was recognized as an Editors' Prize Commended Poem in Magma Journal's 2019 competition. A Midwesterner by birth and at heart, she lives in Portland, Oregon.

Sylvia Sukop completed her MFA at Washington University in St. Louis in 2018 and her work has appeared in *Waxwing, Exposure,* and other publications. She teaches creative writing and is working on her first book, a memoir.

Alyson Thompson is a queer, black/mixed-race writer & community organizer in St. Louis. Alyson's work centers around healing the relationship with self through the practices of remembering, becoming, & belonging.

Janine Tiffe is Assistant Professor of Ethnomusicology at Kent State University.

Steffan Triplett is a Black, queer nonfiction writer and poet from Joplin, Missouri. He received his MFA in Nonfiction from the University of Pittsburgh where he currently teaches.

April Vazquez is the winner of the William Van Dyke Short Story Prize and Carve Magazine's Prose & Poetry Contest. Her work has been nominated for the Best of the Net, the Orison Anthology Award, and two Pushcart Prizes.

Evan Williams is a student at The University of Chicago.

CPSIA information can be obtained
at www.ICGtesting.com
Printed in the USA
JSHW041102201220
10441JS00006B/42